Helping smokers give up

Guidance for purchasers on cost-effectiveness

Helping smokers give up

Guidance for purchasers on cost-effectiveness

David Buck
Christine Godfrey

Centre for Health Economics
University of York

© Health Education Authority 1994

ISBN 0 7521 0246 X ✓

Published by
Health Education Authority
Hamilton House
Mabledon Place
London WC1H 9TX

Printed in England

CONTENTS

vi

1. INTRODUCTION

Summary

- Smoking imposes a considerable health burden causing 110 000 deaths per year in the UK. It also imposes a substantial economic burden, costing over £1.2 bn in terms of health care resources in England and Wales every year.
- *The Health of the Nation* has set targets for cigarette smoking to decline by one-third by the turn of the century. There are many possible strategies to meet these targets including tax and advertising policies and smoking prohibition policies in public places.
- However, the main focus of this report is to review the cost-effectiveness of smoking cessation health education interventions. The purchase of cessation interventions is the main option for health service purchasers at a local level and guidance is needed in securing value for money from their expenditure.
- This report provides purchasers with an up-to-date review and analysis of the most cost-effective interventions for smoking cessation.
- Chapter 1 gives guidance on how to carry out an economic evaluation and critically evaluate and interpret the cost-effectiveness results from other studies.

1. Introduction

There has been a dramatic decline in the numbers smoking since the first reports on the harmful effects of tobacco smoke were published in the late 1950s and early 1960s. Despite these changes in behaviour, tobacco use is one of the major causes of mortality, accounting for 110 000 premature deaths among smokers annually in the UK, 92 000 of these in England (Callum *et al.*, 1992). More recently attention has also been focused on the threat to life and health of non-smokers from passive smoking. Reducing the numbers smoking would bring a large health benefit to the population. *The Health of the Nation* white paper (Department of Health, 1992a) includes targets to reduce smoking by one-third by the year 2000.

There is a range of policies which could be used to achieve these targets. Tax, advertising controls and restrictions on smoking in the workplace and public places would contribute to achieving target reductions in smoking. Health education and promotion initiatives could not only provide support for these types of change but also directly influence the numbers starting and quitting smoking. These initiatives, at a local and national level, however, involve scarce health promotion resources. Purchasers of health promotion are faced by questions on how best to allocate their budgets to achieve the maximum health benefits and those providing health promotion want to demonstrate that their activities are worth while.

The purpose of this report is:

- to examine available evidence on the cost-effectiveness of different types of smoking cessation intervention;
- to develop criteria to assess the relevance of available research to policy decisions;
- to provide some examples of how economic analysis may aid decision making at a local or national level.

The report forms part of a wider project which has been examining the issues arising from applying an economic framework to health promotion activities. This report can therefore be seen in the wider context of applying economic evaluation techniques to a risk factor. More detail on the principles of the economic evaluation of health promotion activities are contained in Tolley (1993) and the application of the economic framework to a disease, namely coronary heart disease, is considered in Buck *et al.* (1994).

2. The health and economic burden of smoking

The health burden of smoking includes premature death, smoking-related disability and illness. As well as affecting the quantity and quality of life of smokers there are considerable health effects on those working or living with smokers. The effects on the unborn and children, especially those with conditions such as asthma, are of particular concern. Compared to the Great Britain average of 28 per cent, rates of smoking were higher in the North (31 per cent) and the North West (30 per cent) and lower in the East Midlands (25 per cent) and the South West (25 per cent), in 1992. Part of this variation can be explained by demographic and economic factors. The unemployed and those in unskilled manual occupations have much higher rates of smoking than average, see *General Household Survey 1992* (OPCS, 1994). There may, therefore, be a rationale for selective targeting of health education at such groups. Targeting is discussed in more depth in the following chapters.

Despite the general decline in smoking, continued tobacco consumption creates a considerable health and economic burden for the population and successful action to reduce smoking is one of the major means of improving the health of a large section of the population. The detrimental health effects of smoking have been well documented. Data on premature mortality are the most comprehensive. Smoking-related deaths account for 18 per cent of all deaths in the UK (Callum *et al.*, 1992) and a third of deaths occurring in middle age (Townsend, 1993). Of the total smoking-related deaths in 1988, 29 per cent were due to lung cancer, 29 per cent due to heart disease, 20 per cent due to chronic obstructive pulmonary disease and 10 per cent due to other cancers (Callum *et al.*, 1992).

The risks of dying from a smoking-related disease are related to the time period a person has smoked and the amount smoked but the exact relationship varies with disease. This is reflected, for example, in the time trends in lung cancer deaths which have been falling for men over the period 1970 to 1990 but which were rising for women until 1989 (Department of Health, 1992a). There is elevated risk (although substantially reduced) of developing lung cancer in ex-smokers even after 15 years of cessation compared to those who have never smoked (Townsend, 1993). Changes to heart disease rates are likely to be more rapid with the risks of ex-smokers reverting to those of non-smokers after five years. Current levels of smoking-related deaths therefore reflect past smoking habits and there will be a time lag between reductions in smoking and reductions in all smoking-related diseases.

Comprehensive data on smoking-related morbidity are more difficult to compile. Smoking-related diseases have been calculated to be responsible for an extra 450 000 hospital admissions each year which translates into a cost to the health service for inpatient treatment of between £261m and £400m for England and Wales in 1990/1 prices (Callum *et al.*, 1992; Godfrey *et al.*, 1993). Smokers also visit their GPs more often, obtain more prescriptions and make greater use of outpatient services than never-smokers, leading to estimated additional costs of £89m, £52m and £208m respectively (Godfrey *et al.*, 1993).

Other data on the long-term effects of smoking can be obtained from claims for invalidity benefit using the same disease attributability factors used to calculate inpatient costs. Applying these factors to the survey of doctors' statements for invalidity benefits yields an estimate of 34 million working days lost in the year to March 1991 at a cost in invalidity payments of £328m for England and Wales.★ These figures relate to longer-term health problems. Smokers generally also experience more shorter-term sickness absences than non-smokers. Smoking is related to other problems particularly fires and cleaning and ventilation costs. Fires, especially in the home, not only cause deaths but also have considerable resource costs. Fires known to be caused by smoking materials or matches were estimated to cost £151m in 1990 (estimates from Fire Statistics UK and information from the Association of British Insurers). This is likely to be a gross underestimate as the cause of many fires is unknown. Godfrey *et al.* (1993) also estimate that English and Welsh children who live with smokers incur an extra £143m in health service resources due to the effects of passive smoking on their health. Table 1.1 presents a conservative estimate of £1.2 bn for the annual cost of smoking in England and Wales.

★This figure is derived from statistics for the UK, by adjusting for population size.

Table 1.1: Estimated annual economic burden of smoking in England and Wales

	Total (£m)
General practice visits	89
Prescriptions	52
Outpatient visits	208
Inpatient visits	261
Invalidity benefits	328
Fires	150
Passive smoking (children)	143
TOTAL	1,231

3. Health of the Nation targets

The importance of reducing smoking is recognised in *The Health of the Nation* white paper (Department of Health, 1992a). The targets are:

- To reduce the prevalence of cigarette smoking to no more than 20 per cent by the year 2000 in both men and women (a reduction of one-third from the baseline of 1990).
- To reduce consumption of cigarettes by at least 40 per cent by the year 2000 (baseline: 1990).
- In addition to the overall reduction in prevalence, at least 33 per cent of women smokers to stop smoking at the start of their pregnancy by the year 2000.
- To reduce smoking prevalence of 11- to 15-year-olds by at least 33 per cent by 1994 (to less than 6 per cent) (baseline: 1988).

The achievement of these targets could be expected to yield a large health gain. PREVENT is a simulation model which predicts the changing patterns of deaths that are likely to occur from reductions in risk factors such as smoking (Gunning-Schepers, 1989; Buck *et al.*, 1994). A simulation of the effects of the achievement of the first two smoking targets using English and Welsh data is illustrated in Figure 1.1.

The targets are predicted to save more male than female lives and the health gains would continue long after the year 2000. Translating these gains into life years, the achievement of smoking targets would result in a saving of 54 000 life years between now and the year 2000 and a total of nearly 3 million life years to the year 2029.

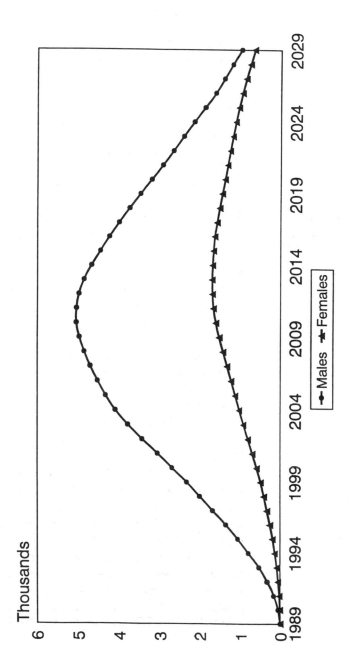

Figure 1.1 *Reductions in the total number of deaths in England and Wales associated with achieving the Health of the Nation smoking targets*
Source: Simulation from the PREVENT model

4. Policy options to achieve Health of the Nation targets

There are many policy options which could help achieve the Health of the Nation smoking targets, involving a variety of actions in different settings and various agencies such as the Treasury, employers, workplaces and the National Health Service.

Price is accepted by both the trade and health lobbies to be an important determinant of cigarette consumption. Current government estimates suggest that a 10 per cent rise in price would result in a 3 to 6 per cent fall in consumption. Consumption is also affected by income changes and increases in real income can be expected to be mirrored by increases in cigarette consumption. Townsend (1993) estimates that a tax policy which resulted in a 5.25 per cent annual increase in the real price of cigarettes could be expected to reduce the number of smokers by 18 per cent by the year 2000, assuming annual per capita income increases at 3.2 per cent per year over the period.

However, different assumptions about the importance of price, changes in income and government tax policy lead to considerably different estimates of the level of cigarette consumption by the year 2000. A sustained tax policy, as advocated by Townsend (1993), may change both the behaviour of consumers and manufacturers (Godfrey, 1989). For example, as the numbers of smokers fall those who decide to continue smoking will be the most 'addicted'. Price responsiveness will fall making tax policy less effective. Alternatively, large sustained increases in price may make consumers more, not less, price conscious. More research is needed on these possibilities. Manufacturers may also change their policies and produce lower priced or generic cigarette brands in response to a sustained tax policy.

Even in the presence of a successful aggressive tobacco taxation policy, other activities will be required for the Health of the Nation targets to be met. Further options include advertising controls, voluntary policies or legislation for the workplace and public places, and health education and promotion. The effects of tobacco advertising on consumption are controversial. The industry argues that advertising merely affects consumers' brand loyalty, it does not make people more likely to begin smoking or increase the daily consumption of present smokers. In contrast health lobbyists argue that advertising has a significant effect on consumption and in influencing the decision amongst the young to smoke. Testing this proposition is difficult and econometric studies disagree about the impact of advertising on overall tobacco consumption and prevalence rates. However, the balance of studies indicate that increasing advertising expenditure does have a small but significant positive effect on consumption (Department of Health, 1992b). There is evidence to suggest that recent advertising bans in other countries have led to falls in tobacco consumption, although whether this is due to quitting, prevention or falls in the number of cigarettes smoked is unclear (Department of Health, 1992b). In conclusion, an advertising ban could make a useful contribution to the Health of the Nation targets although the issues are complex (Godfrey, 1993).

Restrictions on smoking in public places and the workplace have accelerated due in part to recent reports and studies of the ill effects of passive smoking. The effectiveness of workplace policies is open to question however, with some studies reporting associated falls in prevalence but others finding no effect. Also, few British ex-smokers cite workplace restrictions as a significant factor in their quitting decisions (Reid *et al.*, 1992). There is little doubt however that no-smoking policies are gaining in popularity: over 20 per cent of Britain's top 500 companies reported complete bans on smoking in 1990 and 80 per cent have some no-smoking areas.

More aggressive tax, advertising and policies for workplace and public places all have an important part to play in reaching the Health of the Nation targets. However, this report's focus is to discuss the role that health education interventions can play in meeting the targets. Direct interventions to encourage smoking cessation can be divided into two main categories: interventions directed at the whole population of an area, for example, using mass-media campaigns; and interventions which involve face-to-face contact, for example, general practitioners' advice to stop smoking. Although there is a role for advocacy for favourable public policy changes, direct interventions are the main means through which local purchasers and other health service bodies can have a direct impact on the smoking habits of their populations. The purpose of this report is three-fold: to explain why cost-effective provision is important; to review the existing literature in order to guide local and regional providers of smoking health education towards the most cost-effective smoking interventions; and to develop an understanding of the main techniques and pitfalls of economic evaluation in order to ensure cost-effective provision in future.

The report does not discuss preventing smoking initiation in any depth. There are two reasons for this. First, in the long run prevention is obviously the most important element of any tobacco control strategy. However, because of the short time-scale prevention now will not make any significant contribution towards reaching the Health of the Nation targets. Second, and more significantly, with one or two exceptions, specific prevention interventions are ineffective (Reid *et al.*, 1994). They have been shown to delay the onset of smoking during adolescence but in general do not prevent it. However, broad-based media campaigns, aimed at all age groups have been shown also to reduce prevalence amongst adolescents (Reid *et al.*, 1994). These are reviewed in Chapter 4.

5. Why economic evaluation?

Economic evaluation is becoming an increasingly important issue in health promotion and health care more generally. Health promotion needs to demonstrate its cost-effectiveness relative to other health care interventions if it is to succeed in securing extra resources in the future. Within health promotion the cost-effectiveness of different smoking cessation interventions also needs to be assessed if smoking budgets are to be *cost-eff*

allocated efficiently between different interventions. Concentrating on the most cost-effective interventions will lead to the maximum effectiveness for least cost, freeing otherwise unavailable resources to be used for additional cessation interventions. This is the reason for economic evaluation: to maximise the effectiveness of health care interventions, in this case smoking cessation interventions, within inevitably constrained budgets.

The use of economic evaluation techniques and the interpretation of results is a complex area. Tolley (1993) develops a seven-step framework for designing, implementing and evaluating a health promotion initiative. It is primarily prospective, giving guidance on how to integrate an economic evaluation into a forthcoming study. The purpose of the framework is to make decision-makers and researchers think clearly about what they are trying to achieve with an intervention or programme. Of the seven linked steps below, 1, 2, 4 and 6 should be standard to any evaluation of health promotion, 3, 5 and 7 are specifically related to economic evaluation:

1. The definition of the study problem – what is the main aim of the economic evaluation? For example, a smoking campaign's main aim may be either to prevent smoking, reduce the daily average consumption of cigarettes or to increase the number of quitters, or a mixture of all three. It may be aimed at all smokers, poorer smokers or more 'addicted' smokers.

2. The definition of the economic objectives of the evaluation – for example, the lowest cost method of achieving a given reduction in measured smoking prevalence amongst young adults.

3. A consideration of the options available to meet those objectives – for example, the different components of No Smoking Day could be compared to see which is most cost-effective in changing smoking status.

4. A consideration of the appropriate study design – this is important if reliable effectiveness information is to be forthcoming. Ideally this would involve a control group. However, for health promotion this is often problematical because of the practical and ethical problems of isolating the controls.

5. A consideration of which costs to include and measure. Costs are incurred by the main funder of cessation interventions. However, supporting organisations and individuals such as health professionals will also incur costs as will smokers and their friends and families, both financially and in terms of stress and anxiety due to withdrawal. It is important to recognise this when carrying out an economic evaluation.

6. A consideration of which output indicators to use – how is effectiveness to be measured and why? Three types of measure are

commonly used. (a) Process indicators measure the effectiveness of campaigns in delivering the *message* or information. (b) Intermediate indicators measure the effectiveness of the intervention in terms of observable *behaviour* change, for example quit rates or falls in consumption. (c) Final outcome measures assess the effectiveness in terms of actual changes in *health status* as a result of the intervention. Which should be used depends on the aims and objectives of the study.

7. The generation and interpretation of cost-effectiveness indicators (CEIs) – combining cost and outcome information allows comparisons of cost-effectiveness between options. Sensitivity analysis is often employed to check the stability of results when major assumptions change.

Cost-benefit analysis (CBA) is another economic evaluation technique which is less common in the smoking cessation literature except in relation to smoking cessation during pregnancy. The fundamental difference between CBA and cost–effectiveness analysis (CEA) is that the former attempts to value all costs and all benefits in monetary terms. The relevant question then is whether for a certain intervention the benefits outweigh the costs. If they do the intervention is desirable from society's perspective. Results are expressed in 'benefit–cost' ratios. For example, an intervention with a ratio of 3:1 is deemed worthwhile because it produces £3 in benefits for every £1 in costs. CEA on the other hand values only costs in monetary terms, but with a common effectiveness measure can rank interventions according to their desirability, from different perspectives. This is more useful for resource allocation problems where *all* interventions considered may be worthwhile on cost-benefit grounds but because *financial* resources are limited, a choice needs to be made among them.

CBAs are often more difficult to carry out reliably than CEAs because of the intrinsic problems of valuing all costs and benefits in monetary terms. Nevertheless a CBA is a useful tool when many of the benefits of quitting due to an intervention accrue to people other than the smoker. More generally this is known as the existence of externalities. A cost–effectiveness analysis will capture the benefits to smokers in terms of quit rates or health outcomes but may ignore the beneficial effects to others. This is particularly important when carrying out an economic evaluation of smoking cessation interventions during pregnancy. Smoking during pregnancy is associated with detrimental health risks for the foetus. The principal one of these is low birthweight. Several CBA studies have taken the substantial additional costs of low birthweight deliveries into account (see Chapter 3). More detail about the methods of economic evaluation can be found in Drummond (1980).

There are however several issues, both general and specific to the cost-effectiveness of smoking cessation, which are referred to frequently in the following chapters. The issues are briefly discussed below and considered in more depth in Appendix A.

6. Key concepts and issues in the economic evaluation of smoking cessation interventions

The following chapters present and discuss much information on the collection, measurement and estimation of costs and effects and the generation of cost-effectiveness indicators. It is therefore particularly important to have a clear understanding of how to interpret these figures and criticise them. Which types of cost to include is a crucial decision in an economic evaluation since it will have significant effects on the resulting cost-effectiveness ratios.

Whose perspective?

The perspective an intervention is viewed from has important implications for the construction and interpretation of cost-effectiveness ratios. There are many costs incurred as a result of a health promotion initiative and these are not incurred solely by the main funder. For example the Health Education Authority (HEA) obviously spends resources in designing, implementing and promoting No Smoking Day (NSD). However, NSD relies on the support and co-operation of other national and local health organisations, professionals, charities and individuals. In some circumstances it may be appropriate to include only the costs incurred by the HEA in a cost-effectiveness study of NSD. For example, if the objective of the study was to maximise quitting attempts for least HEA outlay. In this case it is irrelevant to consider costs incurred by third parties. However, this would give a misleadingly low estimate of costs if the perspective were that of the National Health Service or the health care sector as a whole. Similarly, smokers and their families also incur non-monetary costs in terms of anxiety, irritation and peer pressure on NSD. The most comprehensive cost-effectiveness studies present societal cost-effectiveness indicators. These attempt to measure costs of all those affected by an intervention, not merely its main funder. Table 1.2 shows the effect different perspectives can have on cost-effectiveness results for a brief verbal GP intervention.

Table 1.2: An example of the effect of different perspectives on cost-effectiveness indicators for a GP intervention

Perspective	Cost per quitter (£)
GP	100
NHS	150
Smoker	5
Society	155

From a GP's perspective the only cost of relevance is that of the opportunity cost of time spent advising smokers to quit. While advising smokers the GP cannot be seeing other patients.* Table 1.2 assumes that it costs £100 per quitter from a GP's perspective. However, from an NHS perspective the costs are likely to be higher due to additional administrative and other costs (an extra £50). Smokers also incur costs, although these are likely to be small, because of the time and possible anxiety caused in receiving advice (£5). Finally, from a societal perspective all costs incurred should be taken account of, in this case, the total of GP, further NHS costs and those of the smoker (£155).

Comparison with the cost–effectiveness of other health care treatments

Several authors reviewed in this report argue that smoking cessation interventions, based on their results, are more cost-effective than the pharmacologic treatment of mild hypertension and high cholesterol levels in middle-aged men. Such claims should however be treated cautiously because there is no attempt to analyse or explain the perspectives adopted or the costs included in these comparison studies. In the absence of similar perspectives and types of cost it is difficult to come to any conclusions about relative cost-effectiveness, and this should be avoided.

Outcome measurement

The measurement of effects is less problematical in smoking cessation than many other health promotion activities. The majority of studies have used an intermediate measure, quit rates, as the main outcome measure. This aids comparison between smoking cessation studies but is of less use when comparing the cost-effectiveness of smoking interventions versus other health promotion or treatment options.

Several authors have therefore used final outcome measures of morbidity and mortality, such as predicted life years gained or quality adjusted life years (QALYs). Because of the nature of smoking, the effects of quitting in 1994 will only become apparent in lower morbidity and greater longevity far into the future for most people. This has resulted in necessary but very expensive, complex and time-consuming cohort studies. It is impractical, expensive and often statistically invalid to follow a group of patients from a small-scale cessation intervention to assess the final health outcomes when more reliable results are available from pre-existing comprehensive cohort studies. All published economic evaluations of smoking cessation which include final outcome measures therefore use existing epidemiological evidence to link quitting decisions with predicted final health outcomes.

In the main, however, most authors use measured quit rates at follow-

---

*This cost is often proxied by the GP's salary. See Appendix C on costing for more discussion of opportunity cost and methods used to estimate it.

up as the outcome measure. Studies which follow up their patients at 3 months post-interventions will have higher quit rates than those which follow up at 12 months. This reflects the inevitable consequences of relapse over time. It is not valid to compare the cost–effectiveness of interventions from studies with quit rates measured at different times. This imparts a bias towards the study with the shorter follow–up, quit rates will be higher and therefore costs per quitter lower.

Twelve-month follow-up is most common in the literature and is most useful for estimating the permanent effects of an intervention, since relapse after 12 months is uncommon. However, concentrating on quit rates is likely to underestimate the health benefits of an intervention if those that do not quit alter their smoking behaviour in other ways. Several studies have reported significant falls in consumption as well as quit rates (Danaher *et al.*, 1984; Wheeler, 1988; Abelin *et al.*, 1989) and an important consequence of the initial tobacco health scares in the 1950s and 1960s was a switch from non-filter to filter cigarettes.

Discounting

Another common feature of economic evaluation is the discounting of costs and health benefits to present values. Discounting is needed to take account of the fact that future costs and benefits are valued at a lower rate than those occurring in the current year. In general, people would rather have £100 now than in the future. This implies that £100 next year is worth less, say £95, than £100 this year. Similar arguments apply to health benefits: in experiments people have been shown to prefer to be healthier in the present than in the future. Benefits occurring in the future should therefore be valued less, or discounted.

Discounting is not possible when process or intermediate outcome measures are used as these do not relate to final health benefits. Discounting life years gained or QALYs, however, has important implications for the cost-effectiveness of health promotion compared to other health care treatments.

Most costs are incurred immediately (for example, a national No Smoking Day) and remain undiscounted; in contrast benefits are delayed and therefore heavily discounted. Prevention therefore suffers in cost-effectiveness comparisons because the benefits from treatment or cure options tend to occur in a shorter timescale and thus are discounted less. The validity of discounting health benefits is a controversial issue amongst health economists. Parsonage and Neuberger (1992) argue that benefits should remain undiscounted, partially on the grounds that health promotion and education options will therefore be more attractive investments.

Several studies discussed in the remaining chapters make use of discounting and Chapter 5 presents both discounted and undiscounted CEIs for comparison. Again when comparing results from two studies it is crucial to check whether the discount rates, if used, are the same.

Cost-effectiveness indicators: their use in policy-making

If it is clear which perspective a study is carried out from, all relevant costs are included and the outcome measures used are acceptable then cost-effectiveness indicators (CEIs) can be generated (step 7 above). This involves combining cost and effectiveness information so that the cost per unit of effectiveness for alternative interventions is known, i.e.

$$\text{Cost-effectiveness} = \frac{\text{total cost of the intervention}}{\text{the effectiveness of the intervention}}$$

For example, assume it costs the sponsor £10 000 to fund a GP to intervene, giving 5 minutes of brief advice to quit smoking to all smoking patients during a single routine appointment.* The average list size for a GP is roughly 3000, of which a third are likely to be smokers. Of these it is assumed 70 per cent will contact their GP during a period of a year and 5 per cent will quit at 12 months post-intervention due to the intervention. Since the total number of quitters is therefore 32 and total costs £10 000, the cost-effectiveness of the intervention is £10 000/32 or £312 per 12-month quitter.

Alternatively, a local advertising campaign warning of the dangers of smoking could cost the same sponsor £150 000 to design, produce and broadcast. The local population is assumed to be 500 000 adults of whom 30 per cent smoke. Of the 70 per cent of smokers who see the campaign 1 per cent are assumed to quit as a result at 12-month follow-up. In this instance 1050 smokers quit at a cost of £150 000 implying a cost-effectiveness of £142 per 12-month quitter.† In these circumstances, the second alternative is more effective and cost-effective, with the greater cost justified by a more than proportionate increase in quitting. If budgets allowed, the second option would be preferred to the first.

However, management decisions should not be made on the basis of simple 'baseline' CEIs like those above. Unavoidable assumptions are often invoked in economic evaluations because of a lack of knowledge about true costs or effects. 'Sensitivity analysis' is therefore often used to test the reliability of the rankings. Table 1.3 shows the effect that different assumptions about the reach of an intervention, quit rates and cost can have on CEIs.

In certain scenarios the rankings of interventions may change. For example, if the media campaign costs rose to £300 000 and GPs' advice led to 7 per cent of smokers quitting the latter becomes more cost-effective. In general, rankings will always change given 'extreme' assumptions. However, an initial baseline ranking is robust and useful if 'reasonable'

---

*Relevant costs include at least the GP's salary, administration costs and overheads plus any materials that may be used. See Appendix C for further consideration of cost categories.

†£150 000/(500 000 × 0.7 × 0.3 × 0.01)

Table 1.3: An example of sensitivity analysis

Changes in assumptions	*Cost per 12-month quitter*	
	Media campaign (£)	*GP Advice (£)*
Baseline	142	312
Media campaign reaches 30–80% of smokers	333–125	
GP advice results in 2–7% quitting		769–227
Costs of GP advice are £5000–£15 000		156–469
Costs of media campaign are £75 000–£300 000	71–286	

changes, or combinations of changes, in assumptions do not lead to a different cost-effectiveness ranking. If this is not the case, managers need to be aware that several options could be comparable on cost-effectiveness criteria.

Cost-effectiveness indicators: not a substitute for decision-making

Cost-effectiveness information should be used only as an aid for decision-making. Decisions should not be made purely on cost-effectiveness criteria. Other factors, such as historical provision, equity considerations and acceptability should also inform the decision process. Economic evaluation is generally used to assess which intervention produces greatest overall health benefit at least cost. How this benefit is distributed has often been treated as a secondary concern. It is possible that the pursuit of efficiency may conflict with the pursuit of equity (Culyer, 1980).★ Ideally, equity objectives could be incorporated into the objectives of an economic evaluation, such as the most cost-effective way of targeting cessation interventions at socially disadvantaged groups. Targeting is discussed in more depth in the following chapters.

In conclusion, economic evaluation is not a substitute for decision-making but an aid. Cost-effectiveness information should be only one of a set of considerations which determine the allocation of resources to competing smoking cessation interventions.

★See McGuire *et al.* (1988) and references therein for an introduction to the theory of equity in health and health care.

Validity of research results

Internal and external validity are also necessary if the results of smoking cessation studies can be used to inform policy choices. Internal validity refers to the extent that a study design reliably measures the contribution of an intervention to any observed changes in smoking status amongst the study's subjects. For example, the internal validity of a local media campaign that took place during a period including No Smoking Day would be compromised because any measured falls in smoking could as easily be due to No Smoking Day as the local campaign.

In contrast external validity refers to the usefulness of study findings in the real world. Study results need to be generalisable to other situations if they are to be relevant and useful in informing the direction of smoking cessation policy. Similarly they need to be comparable so that alternative cessation interventions can be reliably ranked according to their cost-effectiveness.

Internal validity

The major problems found with smoking studies which compromise internal validity are as follows: omission of relevant costs or incorrect measurement of included costs; and the omission of a 'do-nothing' option or control group (see Appendix A for further discussion).

The lack of a do-nothing option or control population seriously overestimates an intervention's effectiveness and therefore cost-effectiveness. Some smokers will have quit spontaneously in the absence of the intervention anyway. This should always be taken into account when carrying out or interpreting a study.* However, with media interventions in particular, it is often difficult to specify a control group because of the nature of the media. Spillovers of information are likely to contaminate results in the absence of rigorous and expensive study designs. In these circumstances second-best alternatives are: to survey viewers (if television) and non-viewers separately† or to use population estimates of the numbers of smokers who quit spontaneously each year. This is likely to be around 2 to 3 per cent (Harris, 1983; Stoto, 1986).

There are also difficulties in attributing effects to costs in long-term interventions. Annual comparisons of cost-effectiveness may not be appropriate in these circumstances. This is particularly true of school

---

*True spontaneous quitting is in fact rare. The process of quitting is complex and most successful attempts are preceded by a cycle of quitting and relapse, possibly involving formal interventions and methods.

†Bias is likely, however, if viewers and non-viewers are poorly matched. For example, non-viewers are more likely not to have access to a TV. Similarly, a percentage claiming to be non-viewers may have seen the advertising, but failed to respond to it and therefore had poor recall. Incorrect categorisation will overestimate the effectiveness of the intervention.

prevention programmes. Flynn *et al.* (1992) report the results of a controlled trial assessing school prevention programmes which took place over a number of years in the 1980s (see Chapter 4). In the first years, although costs were incurred, no significant differences between smoking patterns emerged between intervention and control groups. Over the whole period there were significantly more smokers in the control schools. How should this be interpreted? If taken on a yearly basis the programme would not be judged cost-effective in its early stages. However, if evaluated as a whole the interventions may be cost-effective. The problem arises because the costs expended in year one do not have any *observable* impact until the children become exposed to peer pressure in later years. This is a problem which has not been resolved by health economists.

External validity

Many smoking cessation studies are not easily comparable. This arises for many reasons (see Appendix A), although one of the most common is the variation in the types of costs included in the costing component of cost-effectiveness studies. The major problem with external validity is, however, generalising study results to practical situations. There are several reasons why generalisability may be compromised such as: recruitment bias; self-selection bias; and the lack of relevance of results generated in one setting to another.

All interventions which recruit smokers non-randomly will be less generalisable to random populations, and smokers who respond to invitations to 'register' for an intervention are likely to be self-selected and more motivated to quit than those that do not respond. For example, some studies recruit addicted or highly motivated smokers. Results will not be generalisable to the majority of smokers.

Transferring results between settings is problematical. This is true of some trials of nicotine replacement therapies (NRTs) that have taken place in clinic or GP settings with substantial professional advice and support. In practice, most UK smokers would not receive an intervention in these settings since NRTs are not widely available on prescription, although they are available over the counter (OTC) from pharmacies. Whether similar quit rates will be observed in those who purchase OTC is doubtful.

Impact

This raises another important issue in the generalisability of trial results to practice. An intervention which has a low demonstrated quit rate in a study setting (intervention A) may be superior to one that has a higher demonstrated quit rate (intervention B), because in practice far more smokers will be 'reached' by intervention A than by intervention B. The total number of quitters will therefore be greater and A may be more cost-effective in practice than B. Velicer and DiClemente (1993) have referred to this concept as the 'impact' of an intervention. The impact of an intervention is defined as the quit rate multiplied by the numbers recruited or reached in practice. Impact is a very important factor when considering which interventions to recommend on cost-effectiveness grounds.

Face-to-face interventions can have very high cessation rates, 30 to 40 per cent in some cases, but reach a relatively low proportion of the target population in general.* For example, face-to-face counselling in the Stanford Five Cities project resulted in quit rates of 35 per cent but only 1.3 per cent of smokers in Stanford actually participated in the programme. The 'impact' of this intervention is therefore 0.0045. In contrast, mass-media approaches tend to have lower quit rates but reach a much larger proportion of the smoking population. National No Smoking Days, for example, may result in high exposure to publicity among smokers and a large number changing behaviour for a short period. This could result in large aggregate health gains. For example, if a No Smoking Day reached 80 per cent of smokers and led to just 2 per cent of smokers quitting for 12 months or more, its impact, 0.016, is still 3.5 times as great as the Stanford programme. The key issue when implementing smoking cessation interventions in *practice* is to maximise impact for a given cost. This can be called cost-impact analysis.

There are two main barriers to maximising impact, and therefore reaching the Health of the Nation targets: problems with reach and problems with compliance. Problems with reach include the difficulties involved in implementing successful interventions on a wide scale. Problems with compliance of smokers, once they have been reached, decrease the replicability of study results in real-world settings. These issues are discussed in more depth in Chapter 5.

In general, mass-media interventions will reach a much larger proportion of smokers than face-to-face interventions mainly because the smoker does not have to do anything. A face-to-face intervention on the other hand depends on the commitment and motivation of the smoker to attend physically. One possible method of increasing impact of face-to-face interventions is the routine provision of opportunistic brief smoking advice by GPs during consultations. This overcomes the problem of commitment because smokers would receive interventions when they visit the GP for other reasons. Although quit rates may be lower than more intensive interventions, exposure to a larger population may achieve greater impact and therefore health gains.

Even if reach is maximised, fewer smokers may comply with an intervention than study results suggest in general. This will reduce quit rates and hence impact. This is linked to the problems of generalising study results discussed above. The effectiveness of intensive face-to-face interventions is likely to be compromised with high drop-out rates

---

*A possible exception is delivery of brief routine advice to smokers during pre-arranged consultations for other complaints.

amongst a general population. These problems need to be addressed if impact is to be maximised. The most cost-effective approach may be to reserve more intensive interventions, possibly through making use of self-selection bias, for those that will benefit most and are most likely to comply. Targeting of this kind is discussed in Chapters 3 and 5.

7. Summary of key points of economic evaluation

- In order to interpret cost-effectiveness ratios correctly the perspective must be known.
- Comparing cost-effectiveness between studies with different outcome measures and follow-up rates is invalid.
- Intermediate outcome measures, such as reducing daily cigarette consumption amongst those that smoke, should also be considered important as well as quit rates.
- $\text{Cost-effectiveness} = \dfrac{\text{total cost of the intervention}}{\text{the effectiveness of the intervention}}$

Beware of:

- Omission of relevant costs or incorrect measurement of included costs.
- The omission of a 'do-nothing' option or control group.
- Lack of relevance of results generated in one setting to another.
- Recruitment and self-selection bias.

There are also difficulties in:

- Attributing effects to costs in long-term interventions. Annual comparisons of cost-effectiveness may not be appropriate in these circumstances.

Finally:

- The key issue when implementing smoking cessation interventions in *practice* is to maximise impact for a given cost. This can be called cost-impact analysis.
- The impact of an intervention is defined as the quit rate multiplied by the numbers recruited or reached in practice. Impact is a very important factor when considering which interventions to recommend on cost-effectiveness grounds.

8. Structure of the report

The remainder of this report is split into four chapters. Chapters 2, 3 and 4 review the existing evidence on the cost-effectiveness of face-to-face interventions, cessation interventions during pregnancy and mass-media approaches respectively. Appendix B also lists influential effectiveness studies and this evidence plays an important role in Chapter 5 where it serves as an input to a simulation model. Chapter 5 attempts to estimate the impact and cost of various cessation options by generalising these results to the population of smokers. A computer simulation model, PREVENT, is used to estimate the life years gained and averted mortality resulting from different intervention strategies. The use of final health outcome measures aids comparability between smoking cessation interventions and other health care and health promotion interventions. Cessation interventions are specified as taking place over the course of 1993, reaching all adult smokers in England and Wales. Costs are estimated for each hypothetical intervention. Appendix C discusses how estimates were arrived at. Sensitivity analysis is employed to test the reliability of the results, including relaxing assumptions about reach and compliance. Finally, tentative recommendations are made about the likely cost-effectiveness of different interventions in practice.

9. Conclusion

The prevalence of cigarette smoking has declined significantly since the 1960s. However, smoking still imposes a high health and economic burden on the UK. *The Health of the Nation* white paper recognises this and sets out targets for reductions in smoking to the year 2000. There are several options available to reach those targets. These include taxation policy, further advertising restrictions and health education and promotion. It is unlikely that one option alone will be successful; each must play a part.

NHS purchasers are most able to work towards the targets through judicious purchasing of smoking cessation interventions. However, guidance is lacking as to what are the most effective and cost-effective options at local and national level. It is the objective of this report to provide that guidance and in particular to assess existing cost-effectiveness evidence. This is not an easy task given the few reliable studies in the area. As a result we develop illustrative, but hopefully relevant, cost-effectiveness indicators for ten separate options from a national perspective.

2. FACE-TO-FACE INTERVENTIONS

Summary

- Smoking cessation interventions in a general practice setting have the potential to reach the majority of smokers. However, at present that potential is not being fulfilled: only one-quarter of all smokers in the UK have received smoking advice from their GPs.

- Brief advice from the GP during a pre-arranged consultation is effective in helping smokers to quit. Up to 5 per cent of smokers will quit after receiving brief, to-the-point advice. That advice is also cost-effective, probably costing around £120 per QALY gained in 1992–93 prices.

- More intensive interventions, such as increased counselling, provision of nicotine gum or patches or printed materials are more effective. However, more intensive interventions are also more expensive. It is not clear, from the published literature, whether they are more cost-effective than simple advice alone.

- Intensive interventions may be less cost-effective in practice than study results imply. They require much more time, commitment, and financial expense from smokers in the cases of nicotine gum and patches than brief advice. This will reduce their impact.

1. Introduction

As suggested in Chapter 1, encouraging face-to-face cessation interventions is seen as an important element in reaching the Health of the Nation targets for adult smoking. Such interventions delivered personally to a single smoker or group of smokers can be made in a wide variety of settings such as hospitals, GP surgeries and the workplace. The majority of the literature deals with cessation interventions in general practice and this is the focus of this chapter. However, many of the issues which determine the cost-effective means of stopping people smoking will be similar whatever the setting.

General practitioners in the UK are the first point of contact for most medical advice and treatment and thus represent a vast potential to deliver face-to-face interventions to smokers. They are also in a unique position in which to have an impact on smokers' behaviour, being amongst the most respected and trusted of professionals who have frequent contact with smokers (Fiore et al., 1990a). The recent introduction of remuneration for health promotion in the GP contract in the UK will also lead to more GP involvement in smoking cessation. There is therefore an urgent need to discover which interventions are the most cost-effective and how primary care teams can be persuaded to pursue cost-effective interventions.

The options available to help people stop smoking vary in intensity and cost. The aim of this chapter is to review the existing literature on the cost-effectiveness of the following types of face-to-face interventions:

- brief advice;
- more intensive counselling interventions;
- nicotine gum;
- nicotine patches.

Study results cannot always be easily generalised, resulting in lower than predicted impact following widespread implementation of seemingly cost-effective interventions (see Chapter 1). The important issues of reach and compliance are examined in the latter half of the chapter.

2. Cost-effectiveness of GP delivered brief advice

The simplest smoking cessation intervention undertaken by GPs is the delivery of brief, oral personalised advice to give up smoking. There have been a number of reviews of brief advice and it is clear that it is effective in helping smokers to quit. However, there is some debate about the magnitude of its effectiveness (see studies listed in Appendix B).

The major reviews are summarised in Table 2.1. A strong point of Schwartz's (1987) review is that the component studies were selected on the criterion of 12-month follow-up. Since relapse amongst quitters at 12 months is relatively uncommon (Evans and Lane, 1980), this gives a good indication of long-term permanent quit rates.

Table 2.1: Effectiveness of brief GP smoking cessation advice

Study	*Number of studies reviewed*	*Minimum follow-up period (months)*	*Range of quit rates (%)*	*Mean quit rate (%)*
Pederson (1982)	6	6	3–38	16.7
Sanders (1992)	9	6	2–17	9.4
Schwartz (1987)	12	12	3–13	6★
Viswesvaran and Schmidt (1992)	17	3	2–12	7
Control groups	41	3	–2 to 16	6

★ median

Schwartz (1987) argues that brief intervention by GPs is one of the most successful methods of cessation. In contrast, the meta-analysis of Viswesvaran and Schmidt (1992) indicates that GP advice is ineffective if the 6 per cent mean quit rate in the control groups is taken into account. However, the quit rate in Viswesvaran and Schmidt's meta-analysis of control groups is very high compared to the majority of control groups from brief advice studies, or estimates of the spontaneous quit rate (Russell *et al.*, 1979; Harris, 1983; Stoto, 1986). This is because Viswesvaran and Schmidt's meta-analysis also includes the quit rates in control groups from more intensive intervention studies. In these studies the control group may have received brief advice as a minimum intervention, leading to a higher mean quit rate. It is more realistic to expect a quit rate of 2 to 3 per cent or even lower when comparing brief advice to a 'do-nothing' option. It is therefore reasonable to expect 5 in 100 smokers to quit because of GP advice over a year.

While there have been numerous studies of effectiveness there is only one UK cost-effectiveness study of GP brief advice (Williams, 1987).★ This is a non-experimental study, using effectiveness figures from other sources, and therefore makes extensive use of simplifying assumptions. Williams bases his study on a cohort of 1000 middle-aged male patients, 500 of whom smoke. Five per cent of these are assumed to quit after receiving brief advice to do so during a standard consultation. This in turn leads to a reduction in the annual heart attack rate and consequently an increase in quality adjusted life years (QALYs) in those who quit. The use of a final outcome measure allows comparisons between smoking interventions and wider health care interventions (see Appendix A). The cost of achieving this outcome is estimated to be the GP's salary whilst delivering five minutes of brief advice to all patients plus the opportunity cost of the patient's time. A cost-effectiveness ratio of £167 per discounted QALY in 1985 prices results. The author concludes that brief GP advice to stop smoking is a cost-effective activity even if it only results in 1 in 20 smokers giving up.

Williams's 1987 paper is an important contribution and has been quoted many times in the literature. The study is however hypothetical and some of the assumptions and cost figures are now out of date. As is argued in Chapter 1, sensitivity analysis of the results to changes in key assumptions is important when considering non-experimental studies. The effects of changing some of these assumptions on the cost-effectiveness of brief advice are presented in Table 2.2.†

★There have been several US studies which deal with the cost-effectiveness of brief advice in relation to other interventions. Cummings *et al.* (1989) is reviewed in the next section.

†We are grateful to James Mason for bringing our attention to some of the following points.

Table 2.2: Estimates of the cost per quality adjusted life year (QALY) of brief GP smoking advice in the UK

Changed assumptions	Effect	Cost (£) per QALY
Williams's original assumptions (1987)	not applicable	167
1. Cost figures updated to 1992–93	▲ costs net result: ▲ cost/QALY	285
2. Cost figures updated to 1992–93 1 in 3 males over 40 are smokers rather than 1 in 2	▲ costs ▼ QALYs net result: ▲ cost/QALY	418
3. Cost figures updated to 1992–93 Heart attack rate reduced by 1.4/1000 rather than 1/1000 by quitting	▲ costs ▲ QALYs net result: ▲ cost/QALY	203
4. Cost figures updated to 1992–93 It takes 30 seconds rather than 5 minutes to elicit smoking status information from non-smokers	▲ costs ▼ costs net result: ▼ cost/QALY	156
5. Cost figures updated to 1992–93 1 in 3 males over 40 are smokers rather than 1 in 2 Heart attack rate reduced by 1.4/1000 rather than 1/1000 by quitting It takes 30 seconds rather than 5 minutes to elicit smoking status information from non-smokers	▲ costs ▼ QALYS ▲ QALYs ▼ costs net result: ▼ cost/QALY	119

Simply updating the cost figures implies a cost of £285 per QALY in 1992–93 prices (row 1).★ Smoking prevalence, however, dropped substantially during the 1980s, and a more realistic figure for the number of smokers revealed during a standard consultation is 1 in 3 rather than 1 in 2 used in the original calculations. Given a 5 per cent quit rate this has the effect of reducing the QALYs gained from a cohort of 1000 simply

---

★The opportunity cost of GP time is based on the target salary of GPs in 1992–93 and the opportunity cost of a smoker's time is derived from an estimate of the average household income per adult. More detail of these estimating procedures can be found in Appendix C.

because there are fewer smokers to begin with, and cost–effectiveness therefore falls (row 2). By Williams's own estimate quitting smoking reduces the chance of a heart attack by 1.4 per 1000 not 1 per 1000 as is used in the original paper. For those who quit, the predicted QALY gain is therefore higher and cost–effectiveness improves relative to the situation where costs are simply updated (row 3). Williams also assumes that it takes as long to elicit smoking status information from a non-smoker as it does to elicit that information and deliver a brief intervention to a smoker. In row 4 it is assumed, more realistically, that it only requires 30 seconds to elicit a negative response from non-smokers. This reduces costs dramatically and results in an improved cost–effectiveness ratio.

Finally row 5 combines these more 'realistic' assumptions and updated information. Brief advice may be even more cost-effective than Williams forecast in his 1987 paper! This arises mainly because of the reduced costs resulting from fewer smoking patients and less contact time per non-smoker. The exercise summarised in Table 2.2 demonstrates the importance of sensitivity analysis in checking the reliability of results from non-experimental cost–effectiveness studies. Chapter 5 presents more recent estimates of the cost–effectiveness and impact of brief GP advice using a computer simulation model.

3. Cost-effectiveness of reinforcing GP advice with other interventions and follow-up

As many as 20 to 30 per cent of smokers may attempt to quit after being advised by their GP to do so. However, relapse is common and many smokers return to smoking within a year. More intensive educational interventions can increase the numbers of smokers who are spurred to make the decision to quit and reduce the numbers who subsequently relapse (Russell *et al.*, 1979; Richmond *et al.*, 1986). Follow-up visits to check on progress are also influential in this respect (Canadian Task Force on the Periodic Health Examination, 1986). Table 2.3 presents the main results from review studies of GP interventions which comprise more than brief advice (see studies in Appendix B for more details).

Table 2.3: Effectiveness of multiple smoking interventions and follow-up

Study	Number of studies reviewed	Follow-up period (months)	Range of quit-rates (%)	Mean quit-rate (%)
Sanders (1992)	15	>6	5–35	14.6
Schwartz (1987)	10	12	13–38	22.5
Viswesvaran and Schmidt (1992)	16	>3	13–23	18
Control groups	41	>3	−2 to 16	6

There is little doubt that intensive interventions are more effective than brief interventions in general. However, they are also more costly in terms of materials and GP and patient time. It is therefore unclear whether they are more cost-effective. Green and Johnson (1983) review 43 studies for which enough information existed to construct crude cost-effectiveness indicators. Of the 22 most cost-effective studies the majority combined two or more interventions. Earlier work also suggests that a combination of cessation interventions can increase the cost-effectiveness of the sum of the parts (Lando, 1975; Green, 1977). However, caution in interpreting these results is urged. Costs were estimated in many instances and are restricted to personnel costs in all cases.* Contact time also had to be estimated, at one hour for individual sessions and 2 hours for group sessions, for some studies. The exclusion of other relevant costs renders the cost-effectiveness rankings generated fragile.

The study of Cummings *et al.* (1989) is the only comprehensive cost-effectiveness study which attempts to assess the incremental cost-effectiveness of a follow-up intervention additional to brief advice. The study is non-experimental, effectiveness and cost data are taken from a range of studies, and no original data are used. All smoking patients are assumed to be counselled for 4 minutes as part of a routine appointment and also receive a cessation booklet, at a total cost of $12. A net quit rate of 2.7 per cent over controls at 12 months was derived from a meta-analysis of published studies. The authors further assumed that 10 per cent of quitters would eventually relapse. Results from the American Cancer Society's Cancer Prevention Study are used to link quit rates to final predicted outcomes, in this case expected additional life expectancy discounted at 5 per cent per annum. Again this makes the results more comparable than dealing with quit rates.

Baseline estimates of cost-effectiveness range from $708 to $988 per life year saved for men and $1204 to $2058 for women, depending on age. Extensive sensitivity analysis is carried out with respect to changes in assumptions about relapse and quit rates and costs. Under the most pessimistic assumptions, cost-effectiveness ranged from $5429 to $7600 for men and $9268 to $15 833 for women. Although it may seem alarming that the figures can fluctuate so much, this illustrates the need for sensitivity analysis in other studies and serves as a warning when comparing two studies where key assumptions may be different (see Chapter 1).

More importantly, the authors ask whether a further follow-up visit, to prevent relapse, is cost-effective. The follow-up is expensive because it implies a consultation dedicated purely to smoking, at a cost of $30. The literature suggested that the marginal increase in effectiveness due to a

---

*This may lead to misleading rankings when other costs are taken into account. For example, multiple interventions may have higher or lower than average administration costs and certainly entail more patient time (see Chapter 1).

follow-up ranged between 1 and 12 per cent. The incremental cost-effectiveness of a follow-up visit ranges from $421 to $5051 for men and $772 to $9259 for women both in the 45–49 age group depending on assumed quit rates. It appears that a follow-up visit is incrementally cost-effective for 45- to 49-year-olds, relative to brief advice on baseline assumptions, if it produces quit rates of 6 per cent or more.

In conclusion, although the evidence is far from clear, follow-up may well be cost-effective. However, smoking cessation trials with follow-ups also tend to have multiple interventions (Sanders, 1992). There is an urgent and pressing need for a number of well-designed trials which clearly separate the independent effects of brief advice, follow-up (warned and unwarned) and different intensities of other interventions. At present interpretation and comparison of effectiveness results across studies is hindered by non-standard methodologies and study designs (see Appendix A). Meta-analysis is a potential way of overcoming some of these shortcomings but is not without its own problems. Until more easily comparable effectiveness studies become available non-experimental cost-effectiveness analyses such as that of Cummings *et al.* (1989) and Green and Johnson (1983) will remain suggestive only.

4. Cost-effectiveness of nicotine gum

Nicotine gum was licensed in 1980 in the UK by the Committee on Safety of Medicines and is now also available and in use in Canada, the USA and the rest of Europe (*Lancet*, 1991).

Sanders (1992) summarises the results of 12 recent trials of nicotine gum therapy. In specialist smokers' clinics and similar settings gum is clearly very effective: one-year cessation rates of 31 to 63 per cent were achieved for nicotine gum compared to 14 to 45 per cent for placebo gum. However, Sanders is more sceptical about the value of nicotine gum in general practice settings. Three further studies support her reservations (Lam *et al.*, 1987; Wilson *et al.*, 1988; Hughes *et al.*, 1989). Hughes *et al.* found that '. . . when used in a nonselected group of smokers with a brief intervention in a general medical practice, the pharmacological effects of nicotine gum to increase cessation are either small or non-existent.' Lam *et al.* meta-analysed 14 randomised control trials and like Sanders (1992) concluded that the use of nicotine gum in general practice is questionable. At one-year follow-up, 9 per cent and 5 per cent of smokers, on average, were abstinent with nicotine and placebo gum respectively.

Several authors have suggested reasons why nicotine gum is less effective in general practice. Fiore *et al.* (1990b) argue that gum may not be administered or used correctly. A survey of doctors in the US found that almost half prescribe gum as an aid to cutting down rather than as a direct substitute for smoking as recommended (Cummings *et al.*, 1988). Despite the complicated procedure involved in using the gum most patients are given few instructions and guidelines when issued with it and, in practice, few are followed up or counselled (Hughes, 1986). Headline quit rates reported in nicotine gum studies in clinic settings should not be taken at face value as this success is not easily transferred to the general practice setting. The use of nicotine gum also has substantial resource implications, either for the smoker or the health agency. This issue is discussed further in Chapter 5.

There is little existing evidence concerning the cost-effectiveness of nicotine gum. The only relevant study is that of Oster *et al.* (1986). The authors consider the cost-effectiveness of an intervention in a hypothetical group of 250 patients who receive advice and a prescription for nicotine gum in a primary care setting. In common with most other smoking cessation cost-effectiveness studies it is non-experimental, gathering effectiveness and cost information from other studies. The study links quit rates to final health outcomes by means of epidemiological evidence on life expectancies of smokers and non-smokers, which increases the comparability of cost-effectiveness between this and other health care treatments.

In brief, 4.5 per cent of smokers are assumed to quit and remain abstinent to one year as a result of brief advice alone and a further 1.6 per cent as a result of receiving nicotine gum.*† Although all 250 hypothetical patients receive a prescription for gum the authors assume a compliance rate of only 25 per cent. Of 63 users, 4 will be abstinent at one year compared to only 3 because of GPs' advice alone. Therefore of a total of 250 patients, 12 rather than 11 will have quit due to the use of nicotine gum. Costs include 5 minutes of GPs' time to deliver a prescription and advice and the costs of 4 months' supply of gum for successful quitters and 1 months' for unsuccessful users. Although it is not explicitly stated in the paper it is implied that all costs reported are in 1984 dollars. A 5 per cent discount rate is applied.

The cost per life year saved for smokers aged 35 to 69 is reported. It is more cost-effective to treat males rather than females: $4113 to $6465 per life year saved as opposed to $6880 to $9473 respectively, and those in the 45–54 age-range rather than older smokers. This is similar to the result of Cummings *et al.* (1989). There are several reasons for these findings. First, women tend to suffer fewer adverse consequences of smoking than males. Cessation will therefore yield relatively fewer health benefits and therefore cost-effectiveness will fall. Second, although the benefits to younger smokers are higher, they occur farther into the future than for middle-aged smokers and are discounted to a higher degree, thus reducing cost-effectiveness. Third, for older smokers, expected benefits, although occurring sooner, will not lead to substantial increases in life-years saved because of death from competing causes.

---

*The figure for brief advice (95 per cent CI: 4–5.1 per cent) resulted from a meta-analysis of English language sources and differs markedly from the figure of 2.7 per cent (95 per cent CI: 1–4.4 per cent) in Cummings *et al.* (1989).

†The effectiveness of gum was calculated as the weighted average of cessation rates in randomised trials of nicotine to placebo gum multiplied by the previously calculated brief advice rate.

The policy implications of these results may seem clear: males should receive priority over females and middle-aged smokers should receive priority over other age groups. However, cost-effectiveness should not be the only criterion for deciding who should be treated. Equity considerations are another important factor to be taken into account: prioritising males over females according to such an inflexible rule can be argued to be discrimination. Cost-effectiveness indicators (CEIs) need to be interpreted cautiously and weighed against other legitimate objectives of decision-makers (see Chapter 1).

The authors subjected their results to a comprehensive sensitivity analysis, examining the effects on their conclusions of changes in key assumptions. The largest impact on the cost-effectiveness figures is the pessimistic assumption that nicotine gum is virtually ineffectual in addition to physicians' advice. Realistic changes in other assumptions do not alter the cost-effectiveness statistics to any great degree. They conclude that nicotine gum therapy compares well with other long-accepted medical practices such as the pharmacological treatment of mild hypertension in middle-aged men ($11 300 per life year saved) and treatment of high cholesterol levels in the same group ($126 000 per life year saved). However, before comparisons such as these should be made it needs to be shown that the range of costs included in each study are truly comparable and that discounting and sensitivity procedures have been standardised across the studies (see Chapter 1).

There are also a number of methodological problems with the paper. The most serious is the method of estimating the effectiveness of nicotine gum as an adjunct to advice. The authors argue that the setting has little effect on cessation rates, even though the studies used in calculating the effectiveness of nicotine gum in relation to placebo gum were mainly based in smoking cessation clinics. This is likely to result in an overestimate of the effectiveness of nicotine gum in the GP setting. Conversely, multiplying the resulting ratio by the figure for brief advice will tend to underestimate the effectiveness of nicotine gum, if the effectiveness of placebo gum is greater than the naturally occurring quit rate. Since the cost-effectiveness results of Oster *et al.* (1986) are most sensitive to the assumed additional effectiveness of nicotine gum, they should be treated with some caution.

5. Cost-effectiveness of transdermal nicotine patches

Transdermal nicotine patches (TNPs) are the most popular alternative to nicotine gum and were designed to overcome its reported compliance problems. Approval in 1992 by the US Food and Drug Administration has been accompanied by an unprecedented marketing campaign urging smokers to consult their physicians about the patch (Fiore *et al.*, 1992), resulting in US sales of more than $1 billion in 1992 (Hwang and Lee, 1992). A similar high-profile marketing campaign has recently begun in the UK.

Several recent studies have shown that TNPs are at least as effective as nicotine gum in clinic settings (Tønneson *et al.*, 1991; Transdermal Nicotine Study Group, 1991) and a major three-year trial is to be launched by the European Respiratory Society in 1994 to evaluate the effectiveness of TNPs on nicotine-dependent smokers in Europe (Owen, 1992). Whether patches are as effective, or cost-effective, in general practice and non-medical settings urgently needs to be assessed.

Abelin *et al.* (1989) randomised 199 smokers from 21 Swiss general practices to treatment (24-hour TNP) or placebo control during the 12-week course. However, all were long-term smokers and highly motivated to stop. This reduces the generalisability of the results to more general, less-motivated populations. Total abstinence was also urged but 1 to 3 cigarettes weekly and a measured carbon monoxide content of less than 12 parts per million in expired air was defined as abstinent.

Twenty of the subjects dropped out or were lost to follow-up in the nicotine group and 21 in the placebo group at 3 months (20 per cent); all were counted as smokers. Verified abstinence rates at 1, 2 and 3 months were recorded as 41, 36 and 36 per cent (nicotine patch) and 19, 20 and 23 per cent (placebo patch) respectively. These results compare well with trials of nicotine gum versus placebo gum in general practice where effectiveness is questionable. Quit rates are similar to those attained by gum trials in smoking clinic settings but without the extensive and expensive psychological support.

However, other studies have shown that abstinence rates drop quite dramatically over longer periods. The study of Tønnesen *et al.* (1991), although clinic-based, was designed to be minimally invasive with no group support or counselling. One lapse, defined as unlimited smoking for up to 24 hours followed by smoking less than 15 per cent of normal intake, was allowed between every two visits. Visits took place at 1, 3, 6, 12, 26 and 52 weeks and abstinence was measured at all visits from 6 weeks – 53, 41, 24 and 17 per cent (TNP) and 17, 10, 5 and 4 per cent (placebo) quit rates were recorded respectively. The more conservative outcome measure (total abstinence for 12 and 52 weeks) yielded respective quit rates of 26 and 11 per cent in the nicotine group and 3 and 2 per cent in the placebo group. Although comparing the two studies is difficult because of methodological differences and settings it is not unreasonable to suppose that a similar pattern of relapse is likely to hold in the general practice setting.

Fiore *et al.* (1992) also find that although TNPs' short-term effectiveness is universally high abstinence rates at six months and more are markedly lower. This affirms the importance of relapse prevention in any effective cessation treatment. The authors argue that the TNP suffers from few of the disadvantages faced by use of nicotine gum in a general practice setting but point out the critical role of adjuvant therapy in success: quit rates are much higher when incorporated into a formal cessation programme. In the United States there are many readily accessible adjuvant materials designed for physicians and their patients.

The four American brands of TNP (Habitrol, Nicoderm, Nicotrol, and Prostep) also contain quite comprehensive cessation information and advice within the pack. Existing trials do not indicate whether subjects have access to such information during the trial. If they do the independent effects of patches may be overestimated.

A criticism of existing TNP studies is that abstention is rather loosely defined. This can lead to misleadingly good headline quit rates which are not directly comparable with studies analysing other methods of smoking cessation. In the UK the effectiveness of patches may be undermined because patches are sold over the counter (OTC) (Saul, 1993). This is in sharp contrast to the position in the United States, where physicians must prescribe patches and therefore provide additional advice and support. Because of the marketing position of nicotine patches in the UK such support will not be received by the majority of users. As Saul concludes, whether the gains from the patches' widespread OTC availability will make up for its reduced effectiveness in non-medical settings remains to be seen.

The OTC debate may also have further ramifications. Kabia, the manufacturers of Nicorette, recommend a three-month course of treatment, and a smoker who follows this advice will incur total costs of £103.68 over that period.* The high cost of private purchase may discriminate against motivated but poorer smokers. Whilst as yet there are no studies for TNPs, Cox and Mckenna (1990) found that where nicotine gum was provided by the employer there was a significantly higher one-year cessation rate than among those who had to purchase gum themselves. Hughes *et al.* (1991) reach similar conclusions in their study of smokers from a family practice randomly assigned to pay $20, $6 and $0 a box.

No studies of the cost-effectiveness of nicotine patches, in whatever setting, have yet been published. However, given the complexities discussed above it is doubtful that results from clinic settings will be relevant to the general practice or OTC sales. The costs to health agencies will be lower in these settings but because of the lack of intensive support effectiveness will also be compromised. Compliance problems are likely to be accentuated by high personal costs to smokers, the inconvenience of continued use and possible side effects.

6. Cost-effectiveness and impact of GP smoking cessation interventions in practice

Most studies of GP smoking cessation interventions have been carried out on a small scale in controlled environments. This maximises internal validity but at a cost in terms of the generalisability of the results. The important question for policy-makers is whether interventions will be cost-effective, and have a worthwhile impact, in practice (see Chapter 1).

*Prescribing and cost information from a Nicorette advertisement, classified advertisements section, *British Medical Journal*, 28 November 1992. Saul (1993) reports a higher range of £147 to £183 for a full course of one of the licensed brands in the UK – Nicotinell, Nicabate and Nicorette.

This section discusses methods of overcoming two potential barriers to cost–effectiveness and impact: implementation and compliance.

Implementation

Many of the studies reviewed above and listed in Appendix B recommend the routine delivery of smoking cessation interventions by GPs. However, this is naive, as relatively few GPs have actually delivered routine smoking cessation interventions in the past (Dickinson *et al.*, 1989). This lack of involvement can be explained by several factors including the fact that GPs are generally not reimbursed for the time spent counselling patients and that many GPs in the UK and USA still believe that their advice is not worthwhile (Wells *et al.*, 1986). For example, only 3 per cent of American physicians thought that they were 'very successful' in helping patients with smoking cessation (Weshler *et al.*, 1983).

However, it is likely that even brief GP advice would be cost-effective if it became a routine procedure with all smokers (see section 2). Getting GPs to implement that advice is therefore very important. The new GP health promotion bandings are a major step forward in this respect, committing GPs to delivering cessation interventions where appropriate. It is therefore important not only to find which interventions are most cost-effective but also to maximise the effectiveness and cost-effectiveness of GPs in delivering those interventions. The bandings system needs to be monitored and evaluated closely to ensure that it meets its goals on smoking cessation.

Several studies have assessed the effectiveness of reminding GPs to give advice and educating them to do so. Cohen *et al.* (1989) found that simply attaching stickers to the cover of patients' notes increases advice giving and cessation. McPhee *et al.* (1991) report similar results from computer-generated reminders. Duncan *et al.* (1991) have shown that even brief cessation training increases GPs' advice rates. However, training GPs and getting them to deliver advice is not costless.

Cockburn *et al.* (1992) report an investigation into the cost-effectiveness of three approaches for marketing smoking cessation programmes to Australian GPs. Although it is not explicitly stated whose perspective is being considered it appears, from the lack of consideration of patient and GP costs, to be that of an outside sponsoring body, the Victorian Health and Smoking Program.

The study was based on 264 randomly selected GPs in actual settings in Melbourne, so increasing generalisability. A specially designed cessation kit was randomly marketed in three ways: (a) personal delivery to the GP and presentation by an educational facilitator about the kit and a signed letter from a well-known anti-smoking activist; (b) delivery to the practice receptionist by volunteer courier who also delivered the letter and explained the importance of the GP using the kit; and (c) postal delivery to the practice. Follow-up to reinforce the impact of the kit took place six weeks later for all three approaches but differed according to marketing method: (a) personal visit; (b) phone call; and (c) letter.

Effectiveness was defined in terms of the use and acceptance of the kit by the GP. A research assistant visited each practice after four months and asked GPs to fill in a questionnaire about its ease of use, informativeness and acceptability. Phone calls and letters were also sent to maximise returns. The overall return rate was 79 per cent and did not differ significantly among marketing approaches. GPs faced with the educational facilitator approach were significantly more likely to have seen the kit (99 per cent) than GPs who were mailed or visited by the courier, and were also more likely to use the contact cards. Use of other components was similar between the groups.

Costs were only mentioned cursorily in this study and covered staff training, salary, clerical, travel, phone and postage expenses. The most serious omission is the market value of the volunteer courier used in approach (b). The exclusion of such costs is debatable since routine replications of the study would not necessarily use volunteer labour, and cost-effectiveness figures, and possibly rankings, could change considerably if paid labour were utilised in option (b). Overheads were also excluded. The cost per GP for each of the three marketing strategies was presented. The educational facilitator was far more expensive (A$142) than the volunteer courier (A$14) or mail (A$6). The authors conclude that the educational facilitator and volunteer courier approaches were not cost-effective due to the high costs of implementation relative to postage delivery.

This cost-effectiveness study is dissatisfying for several reasons. First, the exclusion of courier costs biases the cost per GP figures. Second, the process indicator used in the cost-effectiveness calculation is very narrow. Cost per GP is a valid indicator of the cost-effectiveness of the three approaches in contacting GPs about the intervention. However, the authors spend considerable time discussing the effect that different marketing strategies have on their principle concern, acceptance and use of the kit, only to ignore the important cost-effectiveness issues relating to use. It would have been easy to construct more relevant indicators such as: cost per GP who used at least one resource; cost per full kit used; and cost per item distributed to patients. Third, the large number of variables reduces internal validity. Fourth, the volunteer courier over-zealously explained the importance of the kit to 26 per cent of GPs in person, thereby contaminating the results. Fifth, there is no sensitivity analysis.

Despite these problems, the study does show indirectly, that mailing such kits to GPs is probably the most cost-effective method of marketing since effectiveness, defined in terms of use of the kit, differs little between strategies and the costs of the other approaches arc 14- and 142-fold greater.

In a similar vein, McParlane *et al.* (1987) report the results of a quasi-experimental community trial to market smoking and pregnancy education materials to private practice physicians in Houston, Texas. In this case the perspectives are explicitly stated as those of a voluntary health organisation (VHO) and society. Twenty-four eligible practitioners were visited for 20 minutes by a volunteer who stressed the importance of the intervention and offered the materials at $20 per kit. Thirteen of the 24 purchased the kit, 9 of these used the materials as recommended.

Personnel, transport, supplies, materials, physician and proxy volunteer costs were calculated and cost/visit, cost/kit purchased, cost/physician using materials as recommended and cost/potential kit distributed to patients cost-effectiveness ratios presented. The VHO's costs are much lower because of the exclusion of physician and volunteer time and the cost of education materials. Society as a whole, however, must incur the burden of all these costs and consequently its cost-effectiveness ratios are three times that of the health agency's (see Table 2.4). This illustrates an important point in the economic evaluation of health promotion: the perspective taken is instrumental in determining the broad magnitude of costs and therefore cost-effectiveness ratios. When comparing results from different studies it is crucial to ensure that the perspectives behind the figures are similar if not identical (see Chapter 1).

Table 2.4: Cost–effectiveness ratios of outreach strategies to private physicians

Study	Sample	Response rate (%)	Cost-effectiveness ratios	
			Society ($)	Agency ($)
McParlane *et al.* (1987)				
(a) cost per visit	35	69	50.52	16.36
(b) cost per buy	35	27	94.36	30.55

Source: Derived from McParlane *et al.* (1987).

The existing studies of the cost-effectiveness of implementing cessation interventions are of non-UK origin. In consequence they address the cost-effectiveness of marketing interventions, normally discrete 'kits', to individual physicians or practices. Little analysis is made of the impact on the subsequent use of the intervention or its impact on cessation. These are serious limitations. In the UK the situation is much different. Although there may be a role for more commercial approaches the major mechanism for implementation will be through the new health promotion bandings system. The responsibility for successful implementation of cost-effective smoking interventions lies with Family Health Services Authorities (FHSAs). The potential of GP interventions has not yet been fulfilled: fewer than 1 in 3 smokers said they had ever been advised to quit by their GP in 1990 (Reid *et al.*, 1992). Even with quit rates of 5 per cent brief advice could be a cost-effective means of smoking cessation because of its potential for yielding large eventual health gains in the population, if integrated into routine visits to the GP. Such advice would overcome one of the main difficulties with smoking cessation programmes: their low exposure to the target population. Such advice in the general practice setting has the potential to reach a much larger proportion of the smoking population than clinic, community or hospital-based interventions.

However, in practice there are significant barriers to widespread implementation. This is particularly true of more intensive interventions which although more effective under trial conditions are likely to be very resource intensive in terms of GP time. They are less likely to be delivered on a routine basis because of the complexity and time costs involved. Other potential barriers include resistance of GPs to imposed and paternalistic policies, the substantial costs of monitoring and evaluating the implementation of policy and lack of sufficient training, resulting in poor and ineffective delivery. In conclusion there are substantial obstacles to duplicating the cost-effectiveness of study results in practice. These issues are returned to in the consideration of alternative cessation strategies in Chapter 5.

Compliance

Even if any intervention, or a group of interventions, could be successfully implemented on a nation-wide basis there is a further barrier to overcome: the non-compliance of the smoker. In practice, lack of compliance reduces the effectiveness of any intervention, its cost-effectiveness and impact.*

It is estimated that 80 per cent of the UK population see their GP annually (Fry, 1993) and there is some evidence to suggest that smokers consult their GP more often than never-smokers (Godfrey *et al.*, 1993). Over 80 per cent of smokers are therefore currently in a position to be opportunistically counselled, however briefly, about the dangers of smoking. Whilst less than 100 per cent compliance will lower the health gains from GP brief advice the vast majority of the nation's smokers are cheap and easy to reach.

For more intensive interventions, however, high compliance is much less likely. Multiple interventions require dedicated and therefore previously arranged consultations. This requires commitment and time on behalf of smokers, and serious compliance problems are likely in practice. In addition the majority of nicotine gum and TNP studies reviewed above are controlled trials that compared treatment and non-treatment groups. Thus the quit rates reported pertain to a group of

---

*Unles the costs of an intervention are solely related to those who quit, in this case they will fall proportionately and cost-effectiveness will not change. In practice this is unlikely since many costs are also incurred in contacting and delivering interventions to those who do not quit. Even if cost-effectiveness was unaltered, impact would fall since fewer smokers would quit.

smokers with 100 per cent compliance to the intervention. This is highly unlikely in a non-experimental setting. Oster *et al.* (1986) assume a 25 per cent compliance rate and even this may be optimistic (Saul, 1993). One possibility is to make them more widely available on NHS prescription. Whilst this may merely transfer the cost from the smoker to the taxpayer Cox and Mckenna (1990) have found that free provision of nicotine gum significantly increases the likelihood of quitting. The issue of economic incentives and smoking cessation deserves more attention.

7. Conclusion

This chapter has reviewed the existing evidence for the cost-effectiveness of smoking cessation interventions delivered by GPs. Surprisingly there are very few relevant cost-effectiveness studies to provide guidance to purchasers (see Table 2.5). However, it is fairly clear that, under realistic assumptions, brief GP delivered advice is a cost-effective intervention. There is also little doubt that more intensive interventions and follow-up are also more effective. However, it is not clear that they are as cost-effective in practice because of the resource consequences involved. In addition, when the practical issues of implementation and compliance are considered, effectiveness, cost-effectiveness and impact of intensive interventions may fall further. Strict targeting of these interventions to those who will benefit most from them may be a more cost-effective use of resources, but more research is needed in this area.

Table 2.5: Summary of cost-effectiveness of face-to-face interventions

Intervention/Details of study	Source study	Whose results?	Price year	Discount rate (%)	Follow-up period (months)	Cost-effectiveness
GP advice to middle-aged males, non-experimental	Williams (1987)	Williams (1987)	1985	5	na	£167 per QALY
GP advice to middle-aged males, non-experimental	Williams (1987)	This report	1992–93	5	na	£285 per QALY
GP advice to middle-aged males, non-experimental: updated assumptions	Williams (1987)	This report	1992–93	5	na	£119 per QALY
Physician advice to 35- to 65-year-olds: baseline estimates	Cummings et al. (1989)	Cummings et al. (1989)	1984	5	12	$705–$2058 per life year saved
Physician advice to 35- to 69-year-olds: sensitivity range	Cummings et al. (1989)	Cummings et al. (1989)	1984	5	12	$433–$5556 per life year saved
Physician advice to 45- to 49-year-olds: follow-up visit	Cummings et al. (1989)	Cummings et al. (1989)	1984	5	12	$421–$9259 per life year saved
Nicotine gum as an adjunct to physician advice to 35- to 69-year-olds: baseline estimates	Oster et al. (1986)	Oster et al.) (1986	1984	5	12	$4113–$9473 per life year saved
Nicotine gum as an adjunct to physician advice to 35- to 69-year-olds: sensitivity range	Oster et al. (1986)	Oster et al. (1986)	1984	5	12	$2042–$50 666 per life year saved
Three marketing strategies for GP cessation kits: (a) educational facilitator; (b) volunteer courier; (c) mail	Cockburn et al. (1992)	Cockburn et al. (1992)	nk	na	na	(a) A$142 per GP (b) A$14 per GP (c) A$6 per GP
Marketing strategy for physician use of pregnancy materials from perspective of: (a) health agency; (b) society	McParlane et al. (1987)	McParlane et al. (1987)	nk	na	na	(a) $16.36 per visit (a) $30.55 per purchase (b) $50.52 per visit (c) $94.36 per purchase

nk: not known; na: not applicable; QALY: quality adjusted life years; A$: Australian dollars.

3. *SMOKING CESSATION INTERVENTIONS DURING PREGNANCY*

Summary
- Smoking during pregnancy is linked to low birthweight and increased risk of death in the early stages of life, increased risk of some cancers and possible learning difficulties.
- Cognitive-behavioural approaches to cessation during pregnancy appear to be most consistently effective. Most interventions take place in antenatal clinics. Windsor *et al.* (1988), in the only cost-effectiveness study, show that pregnancy-specific manuals are more cost-effective than less specific, though cheaper, standard information.
- From a cost-benefit perspective *any* intervention to increase quitting during pregnancy may be worthwhile as long as it is effective. This is because the increased costs to the health agency associated with the care of smokers' low birthweight children far outweigh the costs associated with a blanket smoking cessation intervention for pregnant women.
- It is clear that smoking cessation interventions for pregnant women should be a priority from the health agency's and society's perspective.

1. Introduction

One-third of British women continue to smoke during pregnancy (Madely *et al.*, 1989). The detrimental effects to the foetus of the mother smoking during pregnancy are well established. Prenatal death is 30 per cent more likely to occur to mothers who smoke after the fourth month of pregnancy. Smoking is also linked to low birthweight, perinatal mortality and possibly congenital malformation, cancer and retarded learning. Yet women who quit during pregnancy (even as late as the second trimester) achieve similar birth outcomes to non-smokers (Macarthur *et al.*, 1987). This chapter reviews the cost-effectiveness and cost-benefit evidence of smoking cessation interventions during pregnancy and argues that:

- Because of the implications for future children's health and the large potential health care savings associated with prevention of low birthweight, interventions during pregnancy should be a priority.
- More attention should be given to targeting interventions towards smokers in lower educational and socio-economic groups. Cessation during pregnancy is significantly less common in these groups.

- Pregnancy is an ideal time to emphasise the benefits of permanent cessation. The majority of women still return to smoking after pregnancy. This is a major public health challenge (Brenner and Lielck, 1993). Antenatal clinics offer an ideal opportunity to reinforce the message concerning health benefits of cessation, particularly amongst disadvantaged groups.

2. Cost-effectiveness of smoking cessation interventions during pregnancy

Results from studies of cessation interventions during pregnancy are extremely variable. Sexton (1986) reports abstention rates as high as 20 and 30 per cent relative to controls whilst Lilley and Forster (1986) and MacArthur *et al.*, (1987) report no significant effects. However, more intensive and multiple interventions generally result in higher quit rates (Windsor, 1986). The study designs of some research are also poor. A recent review assessed 20 controlled evaluations of smoking cessation interventions in pregnancy (Walsh and Redman, 1993). The methodology of most studies was viewed as fairly poor on at least one count. Only trials of the cognitive-behavioural type were able to provide reliable evidence of effectiveness. Of these, five out of six methodologically satisfactory studies reported statistically significant quit rates at end of pregnancy. Their results suggest that an extra 4–12 per cent of women smokers would quit for the length of their pregnancy if these sorts of intervention were implemented.

There is only one cost-effectiveness study of an intervention to date. Windsor *et al.* (1988) report the results of a trial of self-help smoking cessation methods in which 309 women were randomly assigned to three intervention groups. They received one of the following at their first appointment: standard clinic information and advice to quit smoking (group 1); standard advice and information plus the American Lung Association's manual *Freedom From Smoking in 20 Days* (group 2); and the advice and information plus a pregnancy-specific manual, *A Pregnant Woman's Guide to Quit Smoking* (group 3). The groups 2 and 3 also received a free ALA information pack, *Because You Love Your Baby*. No further interventions during later visits took place.

Major costs included were personnel costs and the costs of the materials; overheads were excluded. It is clearly stated that the perspective taken is that of the health agency. Although in the study a trained health educator delivered the materials and advice it was assumed that such an activity would be carried out by a trained nurse in practice. Average salary costs were used to cost the nurse's time. At the end of pregnancy 14 per cent from group 3, six per cent from group 2 and two per cent from group 1 were abstinent from smoking. It is not clear whether these are continual or point quit rates. Cost-effectiveness ratios are derived by simply dividing total costs by total quitters for each group. See Table 3.1.

Table 3.1: Cost-effectiveness of three smoking cessation methods for pregnant women

Intervention (group)	Cost per patient ($)	Percentage who quit	Cost per quitter ($)
Standard advice (1)	2.08	2	104
ALA manual (2)	7.13	6	119
Pregnant Woman's Guide (3)	7.13	14	51

ALA: American Lung Association
Source: Windsor *et al.* (1988).

Although standard advice is cheapest per patient the authors conclude that the pregnancy manual is the most cost-effective option because of its greater effectiveness. No sensitivity analysis is carried out although the effectiveness of the specific guide would have to fall by more than half to be less cost-effective than the ALA manual. The authors also present cost-effectiveness ratios from a societal point of view by including the value of patient time in their cost calculations for groups 2 and 3. (Group 1 is assumed to receive the advice in a routine visit anyway, and only those in 2 and 3 need to take additional time to read the additional material. Unless patient time is valued at an unreasonable rate it makes little difference to the outcomes.)

Windsor *et al.* (1988) conclude that standard oral advice about risk delivered in US prenatal clinics is inefficient and ineffective. This is supported by recent findings about the ineffectiveness of doctors' advice in Norway (Valbø and Schioldborg, 1991). In comparison the additional costs of training nurses to deliver a pregnancy-specific intervention would be more than paid back by the prevented health care costs associated with low birthweight babies, the issue which is considered now.

3. Cost-benefit analysis of smoking cessation interventions during pregnancy

Caring for low birthweight babies is extremely costly. Recent cost-benefit studies of smoking cessation programmes during pregnancy have reported that costs saved due to prevented low birthweight are 3 to 7 times the costs of the programmes themselves, although estimates vary widely (see Table 3.2). All conclude that the findings provide strong evidence to support the widespread incorporation of smoking cessation interventions into prenatal care.

Cost-benefit analysis is a useful tool when analysing the desirability of interventions where substantial benefits accrue to others as well as the smoker. Cost-effectiveness analysis concentrates on the benefits to the smoker alone and therefore can neglect additional important health and cost consequences (see Chapter 1).

Table 3.2 summarises the main findings from some recent studies assessing the cost-benefit of smoking interventions during pregnancy in the United States. These studies are all similar in the sense that the benefits are defined in terms of the averted health care costs of low birthweight infants due to smoking cessation, particularly averted neonatal intensive care unit (NICU) costs. Since low birthweight is also associated with poor health later in life, Marks *et al.* (1990) and Windsor *et al.* (1993a) also include estimates of the long-term health care costs saved. However, unlike most other studies the benefits to the mother are not discussed in any great depth. The cost benefit analyses (CBAs) are therefore fairly narrow in perspective, concentrating on the cost consequences for the health agency. A wider perspective would have attempted to value the health benefits to the mother and child.

There is, however, quite significant variation in the actual details of the studies. Marks *et al.* (1990) and Windsor *et al.* (1993a) carried out interventions set in actual practice in health centres and maternity clinics. Results were then extrapolated to a hypothetical cohort of 100 000 and the population of Alabama, respectively. In contrast the study of Ershoff *et al.* (1990) is an entirely hypothetical intervention. The interventions are diverse too. All smokers received a pamphlet explaining the risks of smoking during pregnancy and the intervention group received eight mailed booklets on motivation and relapse prevention in the study of Ershoff *et al.* (1990). The focus was more personal in the study by Marks *et al.* (1990): a hypothetical 15-minute individual consultation, pamphlet and two follow-up telephone calls. Finally, the study by Windsor *et al.* (1993a) was the most intensive, the intervention group receiving multiple interventions and reinforcement at follow-up.

Quit rates fall around the range expected from Walsh and Redman's (1993) review. However, because the intervention in Windsor *et al.* (1993a), did not produce significantly higher quit rates than a previous trial (Windsor *et al.*, 1985) which did not include the reinforcement methods, the authors conclude that they are ineffective and costs associated with them are not included in their cost-benefit analysis. This could be one explanation for the high benefit-cost ratios in Table 3.2. This is invalid given that the groups from both studies are not the same.

The overall costs and benefits of the interventions are given in Table 3.2. However, the studies estimate the benefits, or more correctly averted costs, in different ways. Ershoff *et al.* (1990) argue that low birthweight deliveries incur extra X-ray, nursery, NICU, laboratory and staff costs. This resulted in an average difference of $46 in the costs of delivery between intervention and controls. However, in their cost-benefit calculations they use the updated figure derived by Oster *et al.* (1988) of an extra $366 per smoker. Savings are then derived by multiplying this figure by the number of predicted quits due to the intervention. In contrast Marks *et al.* (1990) calculate their figures on the basis of the average cost difference between 'normal' and low birthweight deliveries

Table 3.2: Cost-benefit studies of smoking cessation interventions during pregnancy

Study	Intervention group	Net quit rate (%)	Price year	Discount rate	Long-term averted costs included	Costs ($)	Benefits ($)	Benefit-cost ratio
Ershoff et al. (1990)	Hypothetical – community with population of 100 000	14	1987	Not applicable	No	4230	13 432	3.2:1
Marks et al. (1990)	Hypothetical – all pregnant Americans who continue to smoke	15	1986	Not applicable	No	23 505 300	77 807 054	3.3:1
Marks et al. (1990)	Hypothetical – all pregnant Americans who continue to smoke	15	1986	4%	Yes	23 505 300	154 665 134	6.6:1
Windsor et al. (1993a)	Hypothetical – statewide intervention in Alabama	8	1990	Yes	Yes	21 600	387 328– 989 920	18:1–46:1

($520) and the increased risk of low birthweight for smokers, as do Windsor *et al.* (1993a).

Despite these differences in approach, all three studies find that the averted short-term costs as a result of a smoking cessation intervention far outweigh the costs of the intervention itself. This conclusion holds after comprehensive sensitivity analysis, except in the very worst case scenario with a combination of very pessimistic assumptions about quit rates, cost of the intervention and risk of low birthweight outcomes amongst smokers (see Table 3.3).

Table 3.3: Sensitivity analysis of cost-benefit analysis of a smoking cessation in pregnancy programme

Factor considered	*Range*	*Cost per lbw prevented ($)*	*Ratio of NICU costs averted to costs of programme (B–C ratio)*
percentage cessation	5%–25%	12 000–2400	1.1:1–5.5:1
cost per participant	$5–$100	667–13 333	19.8:1–1:1:1
baseline risk of low birthweight	3%–12%	6667–1667	2:1–7.9:1
relative risk of low birthweight	1.5–2.5	8000–2667	1.7:1–5:1
baseline case[1]	n.a.	4000	6.6:1
worst case[1]	n.a.	80 000	0.17:1
best case[1]	n.a.	267	50:1

[1]initial scenario, and most pessimistic and optimistic assumptions respectively. N.a.: not applicable.
Source: derived from table 1, Marks *et al.* (1990).

Further, Shipp *et al.* (1992) argue that an intervention would have to cost $150 per smoker for the cost not to be paid back in lower health care costs associated with averted low birthweight.* Even after sensitivity analysis the break-even cost falls to only $48 per smoker, far higher than any intervention is likely to cost in practice, and may be as high as $268.

Low birthweight is also associated with long-term impairments such as

---

*The authors present their figures in terms of cost per pregnant woman; these figures have been converted to a cost per smoker basis to make them comparable with the other studies.

cerebral palsy or mental retardation. Both Marks *et al.* (1990) and Windsor *et al.* (1993a) use US Office of Technology Assessment estimates of the potential cost savings from preventing long-term health consequences such as cerebral palsy and mental retardation due to cessation during pregnancy. For Marks *et al.* (1990) this doubles the already favourable benefit-cost ratio (Table 3.2). Shipp *et al.* (1992) also conclude that had they included more long-term estimates of averted costs, break-even costs and benefit-cost ratios of programmes in practice would have been even higher.

In conclusion any smoking cessation intervention during pregnancy will almost certainly pay for itself immediately, in terms of lower health care costs. Cost-effectiveness is an important but secondary issue.

4. Smoking cessation interventions in the UK

In the UK the less educated and more deprived members of society are much more likely to continue smoking during pregnancy. The study by Madeley *et al.* (1989) of smoking practices in Nottingham antenatal clinics found a striking difference in smoking behaviour between women of different ages, educational and marital status and socio-economic group. Younger women were significantly more likely to smoke than older women as were non-married women and those with smoking partners. Almost 40 per cent of pregnant women who left school at 16 smoked, compared to only 16 per cent and 8 per cent who finished their education at age 17–20 and 21 and over, respectively. Over 60 per cent of pregnant women from socio-economic group V were smokers compared to just 14 per cent in group I. Smokers from the higher classes were also more likely to give up during pregnancy.

This discrepancy in smoking rates and quitting success in pregnancy represents a major, rectifiable public health challenge. It is clear from the American literature that targeting cessation interventions at pregnant women from lower social classes will be a worthwhile use of resources if interventions of a suitable content can be designed and implemented early enough. The only proviso is that interventions be effective.

Disadvantaged groups may not respond to traditional cessation interventions. There is a need for cost-effectiveness studies similar, but with a wider number of alternative interventions, to that of Windsor *et al.* (1988) to assess the most cost-effective method of persuading pregnant smokers to quit, at least temporarily, during pregnancy. Even in the absence of successful targeting the health care savings to the NHS associated with the prevention of low birthweight will be significantly greater than the costs of providing the interventions necessary for that prevention. Li *et al.* (1992) have estimated that nationwide implementation of smoking cessation in pregnancy would result in health care savings of $22 million to $55 million in the US. There is no reason why such large savings could not be realised in the UK. As Windsor *et al.* (1993b) have argued there is an urgent need, and an obvious economic argument, for a series of local or national campaigns to disseminate smoking cessation methods for pregnant women.

5. Conclusion

The case for routine smoking cessation interventions during pregnancy is particularly strong. The expected additional health benefits to the foetus reinforce the health gain to the mother. The costs of instigating such a programme will be more than offset by the averted costs associated with increased risk of low birthweight, as long as interventions are effective. In this sense the cost-effectiveness of interventions is a secondary issue since any effective intervention will more than repay its costs. However, pregnancy-specific materials appear more cost-effective. We recommend that local and national purchasers view the purchase of smoking health promotion during pregnancy as a priority.

4. *MASS-MEDIA INTERVENTION OPTIONS*

Summary

- The majority of mass-media interventions include some sort of televised component, often with accompanying printed materials and possibly supporting events in the local community.
- The great advantage of mass media over face-to-face interventions is their scope to reach the great majority of current smokers simply and relatively inexpensively.
- Most campaigns which consist solely of health information seem to be ineffective in changing smoking behaviour, although this may be partly due to lack of proper evaluation.
- No Smoking Day has been evaluated on several occasions and is a highly cost-effective intervention, although its overall effectiveness is low compared to other more intensive options.
- Community cessation programmes may be a cost-effective option but their success is not guaranteed and a community cessation programme has not yet been subject to a detailed economic evaluation.
- If TV cessation clinics could be cheaply designed they could provide a cost-effective means of targeting more motivated smokers.
- Several studies have evaluated the effectiveness of the promotion of smoking cessation kits. Overall these programmes have had a small and significant impact but the studies are so diverse in content and quality that it is difficult to draw conclusions.
- Media targeting may be a cost-effective option for reaching certain groups whose smoking behaviour is slow to change. More research into the possible use of mass media as a targeting tool is needed.

1. Introduction

Mass-media campaigns can influence smoking behaviour by changing awareness, knowledge and attitudes to smoking (Flay, 1987a). Mass-media interventions are distinct from face-to-face interventions in that they do not entail personal delivery of the intervention. In the UK these are primarily associated with the activities of the Health Education Authority (HEA) and No Smoking Day (NSD). Population strategies can however also be implemented through other mass-media channels such as newspaper advertisements, poster campaigns, leaflet distribution, radio programmes and health warnings labelling. The advantage of population strategies over face-to-face interventions is that they reach many smokers very easily, leading to high impact (Reid *et al.* 1992). Opportunistic brief advice from a GP may reach a similar number but over a longer period.

Mass-media campaigns tend to be evaluated through pre- and post-sampling of quit rates amongst the population or cohort analysis accompanied by comprehensive follow-ups. Cost-effectiveness indicators are sometimes generated. The evidence on cost-effectiveness is categorised according to the framework of Flay (1987a) who conducted the major review of over 50 studies in this area. There are five major categories:

- information and motivation campaigns
- No Smoking Days
- community cessation programmes
- cessation kits
- TV self-help clinics.

The possibility of using the mass media to target interventions at lower educational groups and school prevention is also discussed. Finally, barriers to maximising impact are considered.

2. Cost-effectiveness of information and motivation campaigns

In the early post-war era much mass-media publicity was generated by the various reports of the Royal College of Physicians in the UK and the Surgeon-General in the US on the health effects of smoking. Engleman (1987) reviews the major econometric studies which attempted to assess the impact of these reports.* Despite major methodological and data differences between the studies the evidence supports the view that anti-smoking publicity had a significant impact in reducing consumption. From the perspective of a health education agency, effective 'free' publicity must be a cost-effective strategy for reducing tobacco consumption. A similar argument has been made for media advocacy in a comprehensive prevention strategy (Reid *et al.*, 1994).

However, studies of more recent pure information campaigns have shown that in general they have not led to demonstrable behaviour change. Information and motivation campaigns are essentially educational in nature and rely on the premise that delivering health education about the consequences of smoking is sufficient to motivate smokers to attempt, successfully, to quit. Evaluation usually consists of surveys of increases in awareness of the campaign and its main messages. Actual change in behaviour is less often tested for or found.

Flay (1987a) reviews four information campaigns which produced significant changes in smoking prevalence. However, three of these four occurred in countries where other anti-smoking campaigns were also under way and where the broadcast media were government controlled.

---

*Appendix B contains references to the major econometric studies which attempted to measure the impact of these reports and key mass-media smoking cessation effectiveness studies.

This makes attribution of change difficult if not impossible.* Two UK studies sponsored by the Health Education Council (now the HEA) resulted in negligible effects on smoking prevalence and behaviour (Research Bureau, 1972; Research Services, 1973). The most conspicuously successful information campaign was the application of the 'Fairness Doctrine' to cigarette commercials in the US from early 1968 to late 1970. During this period one anti-smoking commercial was aired, at prime-time, for every three to five cigarette advertisements. US studies have shown that this intense and protracted intervention reduced tobacco consumption by 4 per cent per annum during its operation although data on changes in prevalence are scarcer (Warner, 1977, 1981).

Overall, these campaigns have generally been unsuccessful in demonstrating measured behaviour change. Their main aim is simply the delivery of passive health information. Without additional support to achieve behaviour change the individual seems unlikely to quit. TV cessation clinics may go some way to overcoming this problem, and they are reviewed in a later section. The application of the 'Fairness Doctrine' is one of the few demonstrated successes. This was unusual in its intensity and duration. Without similar political commitment and resources, information campaigns alone are unlikely to be successful in the future. The Royal College of Physicians and Surgeon-General reports appeared at a time when over half the adult population smoked and the adverse health consequences were not widely known. It is unsurprising that they received such publicity and resulted in dramatic reductions in consumption. However, today the social environment is very different, less than one-third of adults are regular smokers and the health risks are known to almost everyone. Simply delivering health information is not sufficient.

Although no comprehensive economic evaluations exist Reid and Smith (1991) present a simple analysis of the possible cost-effectiveness of a national mass-media campaign. The assumptions in the paper are debatable but it was designed as a quick guide to the possible relative cost-effectiveness of different options rather than as a comprehensive analysis. The authors argue that a 'full-weight' national mass-media campaign would lead to 5 per cent, or 750 000, of British smokers quitting within a few months. This assumption seems over-optimistic given the evidence above, although Flay (1987b) argues that media-only campaigns have a similar impact as the American Lung Association's self-help manuals – about 5 per cent. This would lead to around 2 million life years saved.† Total costs are estimated at £8 000 000, resulting in a cost-effectiveness ratio of £4 per life-year saved. There is little justification for the effectiveness, impact and cost figures used, no discounting and no sensitivity analysis. In particular there is an implicit assumption that all

---

*See Doxiadis *et al.* (1985), Hauknes (1981) and Gredler and Kunze (1981) for details on Greek, Norwegian and Austrian campaigns.
†Assuming permanent cessation results in 2.5 life years saved on average.

smokers are reached by the media. Despite this it does demonstrate the potential cost-effectiveness of mass-media interventions, if at all effective, because of their reach – for example compare £4 per life year saved with the comparable figures in Table 2.5.

3. Cessation campaigns

The perceived ineffectiveness of information campaigns spurred research into the effectiveness of media interventions with a specific cessation component, such as cessation kits and TV clinics, and also the integration of smoking campaigns into a supportive social environment (USDHHS, 1991). This coincided with the design and evaluation of several large-scale community cardiovascular disease prevention programmes. Smoking cessation is complicated as most smokers go through a cycle of quitting and relapse many times before they finally give up. Many countries now have high profile annual No Smoking Days. Smokers are encouraged to quit just for the day which adds to the experience of abstinence and possibly contributes to long-term quitting. The cost-effectiveness of community programmes, No Smoking Days, kits and clinics is reviewed below.

Cost-effectiveness of community cessation programmes

The most comprehensively evaluated smoking campaigns have been those set in a community framework. The major problem with this type of intervention is that there are limitations to demonstrating causal inference. By definition many strands of the programme, aimed at smoking and other risk factors, take place in parallel at many different levels and intensities. The studies are tremendously diverse and media content is not standardised. The cumulative effects of a campaign on smoking can often be measured with some confidence by reference to a control community but the specific contribution of each component is often impossible to identify.

In general results have been disappointing, and although large falls in prevalence have been recorded, similar falls have taken place amongst controls. This may be due to 'spillover' from the intervention area but it is more likely to be as a result of natural trends in cessation. The Australian Quit for Life campaign is an exception to this generalisation, where cohort surveys show a significant net reduction of about 5 per cent in prevalence (see Appendix B for references to key effectiveness studies).

Although there are no good cost-effectiveness studies in this area several papers do report enough cost information to estimate crude cost-effectiveness indicators. Farquhar *et al.* (1990) report on the Stanford Five Cities project, an extensive 14-year trial of community-wide coronary heart disease risk reduction. Two treatment cities received intensive cholesterol, hypertension, cigarette use, weight control and physical activity health prevention interventions. The interventions were implemented through various channels including: television and radio; newspapers and other print media; contests; schools; face-to-face counselling; and community health groups. Extensive evaluation through cohort and cross-section surveys was carried out at baseline (1980) and 25, 51 and 73 months (cross-section) and 17, 39 and 60 months (cohort) thereafter.

In the cohort population there was a significant and sustained net drop of 3.91 per cent in cigarette prevalence in the intervention cities relative to the controls at 60-months follow-up. Although statistically significant this is much poorer than some other interventions but has a wider reach. However, the cross-sectional survey tells a different story. Baseline prevalence was much higher (38 per cent) in both control and intervention groups and there was no significant difference between the two at subsequent follow-ups.

This discrepancy is important and the authors suggest a range of general explanations for cohort studies finding more effects than for the cross-section surveys. First, each cross-section survey includes recent immigrants to the city who will not have been subjected to all interventions: only 67 per cent taking part in the final survey had been in an intervention city for the past five years, whereas 100 per cent of cohort participants had remained in their specific city. Second, any behaviour change in the intervention cohort may be intensified by the repeated follow-ups. Those who dropped out of the cohort survey (66 per cent due to emigration) were also revealed to be significantly more likely to be smokers, less educated, younger, non-English speakers and non-white. Over time the cohort seems to have mutated into a non-smoking, older, better-educated, more immobile population exposed to all interventions. The cross-section surveys in contrast picks up dynamic changes in the population due to immigration and emigration.

Because of the differing implications of the two types of survey for the success of community smoking programmes the question of which is more valid arises. Cohort surveys are indispensable for tracking the full potential of a given intervention on behaviour and health in a static target group. However, cross-sectional studies may be more valid in the generalisation of results to other populations. This implies that a campaign in the UK such as the Stanford Five Cities project may not be particularly successful over and above existing health promotion. However, this may be too pessimistic. It is far easier to deliver interventions consistently to UK smokers than to those in California. California has an unusually mobile population, the UK is smaller than the US and the UK's media are less regionally structured. Since geographical mobility is lower in the UK, long-term local campaigns may have more significant effects since leakage to, and inflow from, other areas will be restricted. There is also a greater potential for nationally co-ordinated campaigns in the UK given the crowded population, fewer TV channels and the existence of a national health education body, the HEA. There are therefore arguments to suggest that either cross-section or cohort results are more applicable to the UK. These issues warrant urgent further research.

Although costs are only mentioned cursorily in this paper and no justification and no explanation of their derivation is given, a crude retrospective cost-effectiveness analysis is attempted below. This is meant to be illustrative rather than definitive because of the number of assumptions that have to be made. However, it does demonstrate the techniques that can be used to construct crude indicators of cost-effectiveness. Effectiveness is defined in terms of quitting based on the cohort survey results. If the cross-section survey were used instead the campaign would not be judged at all cost-effective since there was no significant difference in quitting between treatment and controls from this survey. This illustrates the importance of choice of survey method.

Expenditure is stated as $4 per adult per annum excluding research costs and it is argued that this is good value for money.★ This assertion can be tested by deriving crude cost-effectiveness indicators and making several assumptions about the distribution of costs between the programmes. Assuming that costs were spread equally among the five risk factors and that television, radio and newspapers accounted for 52 per cent of the smoking campaign costs, as it did for total expenditure, means that $0.42 per capita per annum was spent on anti-smoking mass media. For an adult population of 84 000 in the treatment cities this represents about $35 280 per annum or $176 400 over five years. Table 4.1 shows the stages in computing cost-effectiveness ratios.

The total number of smokers in the treatment cities (row 5) can be calculated from the prevalence rates at follow-up (row 1), assuming the adult population is constant throughout the period. To gauge the net impact of the campaign requires knowledge of the number of smokers who would have quit in the absence of a campaign. This can be approximated from the information about smoking prevalence over the period in the control cities (row 2). Row 3 shows the percentage change in the prevalence rate in the control cities and row 4 is the prevalence rate in the treatment cities if the change in that rate were the same as in the controls. Row 6 is therefore the number of smokers in the treatment cities if the change in the prevalence rate were the same as the change in the controls. The difference between rows 5 and 6 therefore gives the additional number of quitters that can be attributed to the Stanford campaign, row 7. Because there was more than a media campaign in the treatment cities (for example, face-to-face counselling) we make the further assumption that the number of quitters due to the media component of the campaign is proportional to the media component of total costs (row 8). Costs are assumed to be spread equally over the period of the campaign. Finally, cost-effectiveness ratios, defined as media costs per quitter in the treatment cities are presented in row 10 (row 9/row 8).

Cost per quitter that can be attributed to the media campaign are therefore about $35–$40. This appears quite cost-effective (see Table 2.5).

★This may well be true for the other cardiovascular disease interventions where significant differences between treatment and control cities were found in both cohort and cross-section surveys, but is not proven for smoking.

However, the assumptions about population size and the arbitrary separation of media costs and effects from other costs and effects will bias the figures. The perspective taken is not known and costs are likely to be underestimated from a societal perspective. Community studies need to be designed with an economic evaluation component in mind otherwise retrospective analysis will always be subject to such criticisms.

Table 4.1: A tentative retrospective cost-effectiveness analysis of the Stanford Five Cities project

	Baseline	17 months	39 months	60 months
1. Prevalence in treatment group (%)	28.35	25.48	23.09	20.69
2. Prevalence in control group (%)	26.98	26.98	25.98	23.22
3. Percentage fall in prevalence per period in control group	na	0.00	3.71	10.62
4. Prevalence in treatment group if percentage fall in prevalence per period = control group	28.35	28.35	27.30	24.41
5. Smokers per period in treatment group	23 814	21 403	19 396	17 380
6. Smokers per period in treatment group if percentage fall per period = control group	23 814	23 814	22 932	20 504
7. Quitters due to total campaign in treatment group	na	2 411	3 536	3 124
8. Quitters due to media campaign in treatment group	na	1 254	1 839	1 625
9. Media costs per period	na	$49 980	61 740	61 740
10. Media costs per quitter per period	na	$39.86	$33.57	$37.99

na: not applicable.
Source: Farquhar *et al.* (1990) and author's calculations.

In the UK, Phillips and Prowie (1993) conducted an economic appraisal of the Heartbeat Wales community programme by calculating the costs of the programme over the period 1985–89 and estimating the impact of the reduced smoking prevalence within Wales in terms of reductions in morbidity and mortality resulting from CHD, lung cancer and chronic bronchitis. This paper does not consider cost-effectiveness but is more akin to cost-benefit analysis (see Chapter 1). Consequently the analysis is much broader and asks the general question, whether the likely benefits of the smoking cessation component of Heartbeat Wales outweigh the costs incurred. They conclude that even if only 10 per cent of the recorded fall in smoking prevalence in Wales over the period were due to Heartbeat Wales the economic and health benefits would still outweigh the costs.

In conclusion there are no rigorous cost-effectiveness studies of community cessation campaigns. Although such campaigns may be cost-effective, assumptions are crude and debatable. The analysis of Phillips and Prowie (1993) is interesting because it approaches smoking cessation from a different angle, calculating the minimum effectiveness which makes the Heartbeat Wales programme worthwhile. The next step would be to assess its effectiveness empirically to determine whether the campaign did achieve this threshold. However, a broad cost-benefit analysis does not indicate which components of the programme were most cost-effective or whether all parts were effective at all. Cost-effectiveness analysis along the lines of that developed above for the paper by Farquhar *et al.* (1990) is needed to maximise cost-effectiveness within a programme. A further attempt, undertaking some sensitivity analysis, to assess the cost-effectiveness of community mass-media cessation programmes is presented in Chapter 5.

Cost-effectiveness of No Smoking Days

No Smoking Day (NSD) has a different emphasis from other cessation campaigns. Modelled on the US Great American Smokeout (GAS), NSD was launched in 1984 and consisted of multiple media-related activities from January through to the day itself in March. Extensive pre- and post-sampling has taken place each year.

The immediate focus of NSD is on temporary abstention only. This has advantages over a permanent cessation campaign. First, it increases the likelihood of smokers participating since their commitment only extends to a single day's quitting. This is reflected in the 85 per cent awareness of NSD amongst British smokers of whom over 22 per cent attempted to quit or cut down at least for the day in 1989 (HEA, 1992). Of this 22 per cent, 41 per cent, equivalent to 1.2 million of all smokers, claimed to have succeeded in quitting for the day. However, NSD also acts as a spur to a serious quitting attempt for some smokers, with 3 per cent, or about 90 000 (1 in 167 of all smokers), still claiming to be abstinent at 3 months (HEA, 1992). The impact of NSD is therefore high, despite long-term effectiveness being relatively low, because of the reach of the campaign.

Townsend (1986) conducted a crude but interesting cost-effectiveness analysis of the day based on the post-intervention survey results, epidemiological evidence and estimated total costs associated with the day itself. Simplifying assumptions were used to convert measured changes in smoking behaviour into predicted 'years of life saved'. As with face-to-face interventions in Chapter 2 this makes comparisons of cost-effectiveness with other health care interventions possible (Chapter 1).

The 1985 tracking survey provided data on the duration and number of smokers who gave up or cut down on NSD for one day or longer. The author calculates that 1459 life years were saved by those who gave up for more than a week and a further 430 life years by those who reduced their smoking levels in the three months after the 1985 NSD. This is likely to be a low estimate due to conservative assumptions about the reductions in smoking levels. Total costs of the campaign were stated as £375 000 resulting in a cost-effectiveness ratio of £199 per life year gained. It is argued that this compares well with a coronary artery bypass programme for severe angina (£800 per life year) or heart transplants (£14 000 per life year).*

More recently Reid and Smith (1991) have argued that NSD has the potential to be many times more cost-effective than Townsend's (1986) estimates, at under £3 per life year saved! The authors argue that up to 0.5 per cent of all British smokers, or 50 000 individuals, may quit permanently within a few months as a result of taking part in NSD. Assuming this is feasible, it saves 107 500 life years.† Costs are estimated to be approximately £300 000 at national level and cost-effectiveness is therefore £2.79 per life year saved.‡ The divergence arises mainly because of the discrepancy between the figures for life years saved as a result of NSD. Townsend's (1986) figure of 1889 life years saved is based on more conservative assumptions about quitting behaviour. For example, all smokers that claim still to be abstinent at 3 months are assumed to relapse at 3 months. Thus there are no long-term quitters. This obviously reduces the benefits of quitting substantially. In contrast, Reid and Smith (1991) assume that all those who remained abstinent to 3 months in 1989 did not relapse. The true cost-effectiveness figure is likely to lie somewhere between these two extremes.

There are further problems with both analyses. First, there is no discussion of how the cost figure was derived. It probably relates to the Health Education Council alone and precludes other local agencies' costs incurred.§ Second, some of those who claim to have quit as a result of

---

*All costs and cost-effectiveness ratios at 1985 prices.
†Assuming permanent cessation results in 2.5 life years saved per average smoker.
‡All costs and cost-effectiveness ratios at 1989 prices.
§Including the costs to other organisations, such as charities and district health authorities, probably doubles the annual costs of NSD – Donald Reid, personal communication.

NSD may have quit anyway, and it is not clear whether the quit rate has been adjusted for 'natural' quitting in the sample. If not effectiveness is overestimated. Sensitivity analysis is also lacking, particularly the effect that discounting future life years may have on the cost–effectiveness figures. In Chapter 5 it is shown that discounting substantially reduces the health gains from smoking cessation.

Nevertheless, NSD has the potential to be cost-effective even if Townsend's (1986) very conservative results are the more valid, roughly comparable to Williams's (1987) of the cost-effectiveness of brief GP advice in Chapter 2. If the adjusted estimates of Reid and Smith (1991) are closer to reality then NSD is even more cost-effective. Chapter 5 presents our own estimates based on more sophisticated modelling and updated cost estimates.

Cost–effectiveness of smoking cessation kits

The literature on cessation kits is so diverse in content and quality that an unequivocal statement about effectiveness is unwise (Flay, 1987a). However, they may have a small but significant impact on cessation rates. Cessation kits are usually advertised or promoted through radio, television or the press. Smokers are invited to register with an intervention and receive the kit, usually free of charge, in return. For this reason cessation kits tend to attract smokers who are already motivated to give up. This is an advantage in the sense that quit rates are likely to be relatively high and sustainable amongst registrants. However, it is a disadvantage in that the less motivated smokers, a large sector of the population, will receive little if any benefit. Reach and thus impact may be limited.

Promotion of cessation kits has been limited in the UK. However, an emotional 30-second television commercial was aired on commercial British television during a two-week period in February 1985 (NOP Market Research, 1985a,b,c).★ Viewers were invited to phone for a free smoking cessation pack at the end of the commercial. Surveys of a random sample of requesters and the general smoking population were carried out immediately after the intervention and three months later. Although only 3 per cent of the nation's 15 million smokers requested the pack, at three months 11 per cent of these were not smoking compared to 10 per cent of viewers and 7 per cent of non-viewers. This implies that the kit was not as successful as the advertisement in changing people's smoking behaviour.

Nevertheless, Flay (1987a) argues that for a cost of £750 000 the Health Education Council achieved a cost-effective outcome, estimating that 220 000 viewers and requesters quit for at least three months who would not have quit anyway. This implies a cost per three-month quitter of

---

★The commercial showed a young daughter searching for information on lung cancer after seeing her father – a smoker – in distress.

£3.50. This is extremely low and implies around 2500 undiscounted life years gained if all were assumed only to quit for three months, or 550 000 undiscounted life years gained if they were to quit for good. This implies a cost of £300 and £1.40 per life year gained respectively. Unfortunately no 12-month follow-up was carried out to determine the programme's long-term effects.

The cost–effectiveness analysis of Altman *et al.* (1987) is possibly unique in the area of media smoking cessation programmes. The paper analyses the cost–effectiveness of three cessation programmes from the Stanford Five Cities project, of which one was a smoking cessation kit. The kit consisted of four sheets of self-help material.

Effectiveness was assessed by the measured quit rate of a survey of respondents who applied through newspapers. Unfortunately quit rates were only assessed at a very brief five weeks post-campaign. Unsurprisingly the quit rate was therefore high (21 per cent). The small sample (101) who wrote in for the material is also a problem. The authors argue that the material was also available more widely and actively distributed in the community. They base their cost–effectiveness ratios on an arbitrary 500 smokers who are assumed to have acquired the material. Numbers of quitters will therefore be higher and cost–effectiveness figures more impressive.

It is not clear from whose perspective the analysis is conducted although costs of staff and staff benefits, overheads, rent, supplies and materials, travel, data analysis and participation time of smokers are included. Including the last category broadens the perspective to the smoker as well as the health agency sponsor. The inclusion of the costs of data analysis is somewhat controversial. Should evaluation costs enter into, and therefore affect, cost–effectiveness indicators for the programme evaluated? If the programme is to be evaluated on a routine basis then the answer is probably yes, if not there is less justification. In this case the three interventions were intrinsic components of the wider Stanford Five Cities project and therefore subject to continual evaluation. Costs were discounted to 1981 dollars, the first year of the programme, at 5 per cent annually. Table 4.2 provides details of the analysis.

Cost–effectiveness was calculated by dividing cost at 1 and 5 years by those expected to quit by those dates. A good point of the study is that some sensitivity analysis was carried out: quit rates of 5 per cent to 40 per cent were used. Row 6 reports the cost–effectiveness figures that Altman *et al.* (1987) report for the kit. Cost per quitter varies from $144 to $22 depending on the length of the programme and the treatment of development costs.

This analysis is reasonable, primarily due to the effort taken in defining and collecting the relevant cost data. However, there are shortcomings. The exceptionally short follow-up time (five weeks) and small sample are unhelpful: 12-month follow-up quit rates would be more helpful. There is no mention of the natural quit-rate and therefore effectiveness is probably

Table 4.2: Cost-effectiveness of a self-help booklet promoted through newspaper advertisements

Length of programme	Using total cost incurred		Using total costs minus development costs	
	One year	Five years	One year	Five years
1. Total costs ($)	15 144	26 190	4 698	11 498
2. No. of participants (assumed)	500	2500	500	2500
3. No. of participants (known)	101	505	101	505
4. No. of quitters of total assumed participants	105	525	105	525
5. No. of quitters of total known participants	21	106	21	106
6. Cost ($) per quitter for assumed participants	144	50	45	22
7. Range of cost ($) per quitter for assumed participants for 5–40% range of quit rates	605–75	210–26	188–23	92–11
8. Cost($) per quitter for known participants.	721	247	224	108
9. Range of cost ($) per quitter for known participants for 5–40% range of quit rates	2998–374	1037–130	930–116	455–57

Source: Altman *et al.* (1987) and author's estimates.

overestimated. The authors also assume that 21 per cent of their presumed 500 participants will quit based on a limited survey of only 101 known participants recruited through newspaper advertisements. Whilst there may well be more participants due to dissemination of the kit through stores etc. their number is not known and quit rates may be different amongst these smokers from those who responded to the advertisement. Rows 3, 5, 8 and 9 refer to those who are known to have taken up the kit and provide more pessimistic cost-effectiveness ratios than Altman *et al.* (1987) calculate.

In conclusion, providing self-help material through the media and wider channels may cost as little as $22 per five-week quitter (in 1981 prices). Strictly speaking media cost-effectiveness, in this example at least, is lower. Only 101 people registered for the kit in response to an advertisement in a local newspaper and of these 21 quit at five weeks follow-up. Long-term quit rates are also likely to be lower in practice and cost-effectiveness ratios subsequently worse.

Cost-effectiveness of TV self-help clinics

Flay (1987a) considers the final category in his schema, self-help clinics, to be the most promising use of television. Television reaches a much larger proportion of smokers than most face-to-face methods.* It also allows the use of a sequential, structured programme and visible demonstrations of behavioural skills not possible in written self-help manuals. Since TV clinics have the potential to reach thousands of homes they may be more cost-effective, because of greater impact, than traditional face-to-face techniques. Flay (1987a) reviews 25 clinics, mostly television alone, a few with radio as well, and roughly half accompanied by some form of community involvement. Most studies suffer from methodological problems, in particular the lack of long-term follow-up surveys to determine relapse rates and generate comparable quit-rate data with other studies (LeRoux and Miller, 1983).

Most studies of TV clinics feature some form of registration for supporting materials. From an evaluation standpoint this makes it difficult to disentangle the relative effects of the televised clinic and the printed material. It may be that the material reinforces the desire to quit and thus has a separate additional effect. Alternatively registration for such materials may merely be a means of self-selection of smokers who are already motivated to quit. Extrapolating from study results which are based on registrants alone is therefore potentially misleading (see section on self-selection bias in Chapter 1). For example, LeRoux and Miller (1983) find that quit rates in their registrant and non-registrant control group were 10.7 per cent and 1.5 per cent respectively. This should be borne in mind when interpreting results from the following studies.

The majority of studies in this area are American and report results of clinics aired on local television channels. Best (1980) developed a televised self-management approach to smoking which was aired on six weekly half-hour slots in Washington during 1977. A guide was also produced for those who requested it. All 1400 smokers who requested the guide were surveyed. Total non-smoker rates at three-and six-months post-test were 14.7 per cent and 17.6 per cent respectively, far higher rates than any other study of this sort. Best also provided some cost data, yielding a cost-effectiveness ratio of $48 per quitter at six months.

---

*Routine but opportunistic GP interventions being a possible exception.

Danaher *et al.* (1984) report results of a study consisting of a series of short (five minutes) personalised slots on a local news show at 5 pm and 11 pm every day for a week. Extensive pre-campaign publicity was generated through local newspaper advertisements. Over 20 per cent of the 1.5 million local smokers saw at least one of the slots. Evaluation was by means of a randomised telephone survey and a follow-up of 'registrants': those who wrote in for a programme synopsis, advice brochure and local quitline numbers in the Los Angeles area. Quit rates of registrants would *a priori* be expected to be higher than in the cross-section telephone survey because of self-selection bias and the effects of the printed material.

The authors' main results confirm this expectation: 2.4 per cent of telephone respondents had self-reportedly remained completely abstinent to 12-month follow-up, compared to 6.2 per cent of registrants. Although this study suffers seriously from the lack of a control population the telephone survey quit rates, more representative of the smoking population, were similar to the 2.9 per cent spontaneous 12-month quit rate from a separate survey of smokers in the Los Angeles area carried out by the Community Impact Study Group (CISG) 18 months after the broadcast of the programme. One interpretation of these findings is that local TV media campaigns, coupled with some form of registration option, act as a catalyst for spurring highly motivated smokers to attempt to quit. However, for less motivated smokers, although short-term quitting is likely, relapse is high and media interventions do not seem very effective in yielding increased cessation rates.

The authors also report a crude cost-effectiveness analysis of the intervention which is useful in illustrating the potential pitfalls in economic evaluation. Extrapolating to the entire viewing population implies that 300 000 smokers were exposed to at least one segment of the campaign of which 2.4 per cent (7200) quit. A further 6.2 per cent (217) of the 3500 registrants were also assumed to quit, yielding a rough total of 7400 quitters. The estimated cost of the programme was $200 000. Cost per average quitter is therefore $27. Although the campaign was more effective in getting registrants to quit it appears to be less cost-effective for this highly motivated group than for the others. The additional costs of promotional materials and postage increased the cost per quitter ratio of registrants to $75.68.

It is tempting to conclude that it is cost-effective to dispense with the registration aspect of the campaign and concentrate on a less-specific population approach. However, this would be misguided if the CISG survey is an accurate estimate of the 'natural' quit rate in Los Angeles, since to focus on the population intervention would not result in more quitters than in the absence of any campaign!

The registration option is the only real alternative since it does demonstrate an increase in effectiveness over a 'do-nothing' option. However, its cost-effectiveness is much lower than that calculated by the authors. Since 2.4 per cent of registrants and all 7200 from the population option would have quit without an intervention only 3.8 per cent (133) of those that quit can be attributed to it. The true net cost-effectiveness of the campaign may therefore be nearer $200 000/133, or $1503 per quitter! This aptly illustrates the crucial consequences of not including a do-nothing option in economic evaluations. Misleading and inappropriate policy guidance may result. All smoking studies should either have a statistical control (for example, RCTs) or at least some independent or pre-intervention measure of baseline or natural quit rates (see Appendix A).

In the UK, TV clinics are less common than in the United States where broadcasting conditions are very different. Although cost data are not available, a national TV clinic, 'So you want to stop smoking?', was broadcast on BBC television during January–February 1982 and subsequently evaluated (Dyer, 1982; 1983). The campaign consisted of six weekly 10-minute spots of a format similar to earlier American campaigns, again with requestable printed material and, pre- and post-tests on a sample of 4000 smoking BBC viewers who saw or did not see the programmes.

About 8 million people saw each slot with 2 per cent seeing all six. Quitting was positively correlated with viewing levels. Ten per cent of smoking viewers quit during or immediately after the programme compared to 5 per cent amongst non-viewing smokers in the sample. This last figure seems high, because it may be picking up spillover effects from the programme due to its high ratings, about 15 per cent of the UK population. At 12-month follow-up, 4.4 per cent of viewing smokers and 2 per cent of non-viewers remained abstinent. In addition another 8 per cent of viewing smokers and 10 per cent of non-viewers in the sample were non-smokers at 12-month follow-up, quitting between the first post-test (3 months) and 12 months. Again requesters were more successful than those in the general survey with 21 per cent quitting immediately although follow-up data on this group do not exist.

Unfortunately costs are not reported but there may be economies of scale in carrying out a single national programme compared to many local campaigns on local networks. The large population reached and any scale economies probably makes an otherwise low 2.4 per cent net quit rate at 12 months worth while on cost-effectiveness and impact grounds. Ideally, studies such as this should have had an economic evaluation input at the design stage.

4. Targeting interventions through the mass media: equity issues

Television campaigns and programmes have tended to focus on the 'average' smoker. Whilst this is rational if the objective is to maximise exposure and receptiveness to the intervention it may result in implicit discrimination against certain groups. Well-designed specific campaigns could explicitly discriminate in favour of minorities, such as pregnant women (see Chapter 3). They will by definition reach fewer smokers, or potential smokers, than broader campaigns but could have a substantial impact amongst those resilient to, or relatively neglected by, more traditional face-to-face and population interventions.

Options include targeting existing interventions at specific groups or tailoring interventions to be particularly attractive to minorities. Unfortunately, an in-depth review of targeted interventions lies outside the scope of this report. These issues are discussed below in relation to lower educational groups and adolescent prevention, although they are also highly relevant to discussions about smoking amongst many other groups such as ethnic minorities and young women smokers.

Reaching lower educational groups

A major concern in developed countries is the widening gap between the smoking behaviour of different educational groups (Pierce *et al.*, 1989).* More recently Garrison *et al.* (1993) have found a similar gap in their analysis of Framingham offspring. However, the less educated receive information from television more often than those who are more educated (Roberts and Maccoby, 1984). Use of a mass media-led anti-smoking campaign may therefore overcome resistance to face-to-face counselling or similar methods which either lower educated groups do not, or choose not to, have access to, or are less effective in their case.

Macaskill *et al.* (1992) test the hypothesis that the Quit for Life campaigns in Sydney and Melbourne did not lead to significant differences in quitting behaviour across different educational groups. Subjects were divided into four educational categories: up to 9 years of schooling; a 10-year certificate; a 12-year certificate; and college education. The proportional decline in prevalence for males in Sydney and Melbourne and women in Sydney was not significantly different across education levels, although initial prevalence rates were.

Supporting evidence comes from evaluations of the North Karelia project (see Appendix B), where significantly more smokers in the lower educational bracket were likely to watch the smoking clinic programmes. Unfortunately, as quit rates are not stratified across educational groups, a stronger test of this hypothesis is not possible.

Macaskill *et al.* (1992) conclude that to address the needs of smokers of all educational levels the public health movement should consider using the televised media. As smoking prevalence in society falls and a higher proportion of more educated smokers quit, the characteristics of the pool of remaining smokers is likely to change. The Macaskill *et al.* (1992) study has shown that general media campaigns do not discriminate against the less educated. What is now needed are studies of tailored media campaigns, which actively seek to discriminate in favour of such groups. They may well turn out to be more cost-effective than general programmes alone. This is an urgent area for future research.

---

*The *General Household Survey 1992* (OPCS, 1994) in the UK also shows a clear difference in smoking prevalence between different educational and socio-economic groups as did the evidence of Madely *et al.* (1989) in Chapter 3.

Targeting school prevention

Most smokers report taking up smoking between the ages of 13 and 15 (USDHHS, 1994). School prevention programmes obviously appear very attractive propositions to decision-makers. However, recent research has argued that, with one or two exceptions, specific prevention interventions are ineffective (Reid *et al.*, 1994). They have been shown to delay the onset of smoking during adolescence but in general not to prevent it. However, broad-based media campaigns, aimed at all age groups, have been shown to reduce prevalence amongst adolescents also (Reid *et al.*, 1994). Again it seems that population-based interventions may be a more cost-effective option in general, at least amongst this group. However, very intensive school interventions with media support have been shown to be effective over time (Flynn *et al.*, 1992), but are they cost-effective?

Flynn *et al.* (1992) report the results of an intensive four-year study which compared the effectiveness of a school intervention only with that of a school intervention supported by a media campaign. Thirty-six television and 17 radio spots were paid for and broadcast over the local media. A control received only the intensive school programme. This consisted of grade-specific materials covering decision-making skills, social support and health information delivered by a trained teacher. Grades 5 to 8 received four classes per year and 9 to 10 three classes per year. Ideally, a further control for a 'do-nothing' or usual practice option should also have been included. The relative effectiveness of the programme without the media support could then have been assessed.

Various outcome variables are discussed, the most salient being the percentage of students smoking daily or weekly by year over the period. The number of students who were prevented from smoking can be estimated if the following assumptions are made: the students were spread equally across the intervention and control groups; having smoked cigarettes in the last week is a usable definition of being a 'smoker' and not having smoked in the past week is a usable definition of being a 'non-smoker'; non-smokers will not subsequently start smoking; and the control group is valid. The media intervention was particularly intensive and structured, so costs were consequently high. The cost of finishing one TV commercial averaged $10 369; 36 were commissioned in total. Assuming the radio development costs were negligible means a total cost for the media component of the programme of approximately $623 000 (including average broadcast costs) over the five years, or $124 600 per annum.

Over the first three years there was no significant difference between the media group and the control. On strict criteria therefore the media intervention was not effective in these years. However, cumulative exposure to the media may have made a difference in years 3, 4 and 5 or it may be that the media campaign in these years was simply more effective, independently of the previous campaigns. Which assumption is made has implications for cost-effectiveness. There are at least three possible approaches to calculating cost-effectiveness ratios in this example. They are:

1. The cost-effectiveness of the aggregate campaign – divide total costs by total significant effects over the whole campaign period.

2. The cost-effectiveness of each discrete component of the campaign – divide each year's costs by each year's significant effects for each year of the campaign.

3. The cost-effectiveness of the cumulative impact of the campaign – divide a weighted average of previous and current year's costs by each year's effects.

Table 4.3: Retrospective cost-effectiveness analysis of a 1985–89 school smoking prevention programme with media support

	1985	1986	1987	1988	1989
1. Prevalence in media schools	1.29	1.80	5.01	9.10	12.81
2. Prevalence in control schools	1.59	3.44	9.25	14.82	19.80
3. Numbers smoking in media schools	35	49	137	248	350
4. Numbers smoking in control schools	43	94	252	404	540
5. Number of smokers prevented in media schools	0[1]	0[1]	115	156	190
6. Cost ($) per annum of media campaign	124 600	124 600	124 600	124 600	124 600
7. Cost ($) per prevented smoker in the media schools	infinite	infinite	1083	799	656

[1] Since not significantly different.
Source: Flynn *et al.* (1992) and author's calculations.

In row 7 of Table 4.3 approach 2 is assumed to be the case: there is no cumulative impact; thus expenditure in 1985 and 1986 is simply wasted. The aim of the campaign however was to change attitudes to smoking within the same cohort of schoolchildren over time. The cohort effect is important. Younger children are less exposed to smoking peers at school, and this is perhaps one reason why there is no significant difference between media and school-only samples in 1985, 1986 and 1987. It does not mean the campaign was unsuccessful but that observable effects are only revealed in the later years as successful education results in non-smoking behaviour in response to greater exposure to cigarettes. This cumulative aspect (3 above) is difficult to deal with satisfactorily in cost-effectiveness terms. We do not know what the relationship between cumulative costs and current effects is. This is a particular problem with long-term, non-discrete programmes in the prevention and cessation field. One way round the problem is to concentrate on aggregate outcomes of the programme (1 above). Total costs are simply divided by total effects. In this case the cost-effectiveness of the whole programme is $1351 per prevented smoker ($623 000/(115+156+190)).

Each approach results in different cost-effectiveness figures for the same outcomes. Which method is appropriate depends on the perspective taken and the aim of the campaign. There are some occasions when detailed cost-effectiveness ratios for each stage in a programme are called for in order to address priorities. Similarly a policy-maker may only be interested in the total effects and total costs of the whole programme. In this case however the cumulative aspect should not be neglected since the aim of the study was to promote non-smoking behaviour in a cohort of students over time.

In conclusion, intensive school prevention with media support is effective, compared to intensive prevention alone, in reducing smoking prevalence over several years, although in the short term it is not. It is therefore not clear whether this programme, at least, is cost-effective. In long-term interventions the attribution of costs to outcomes is more problematical. Simply dividing total costs by total effects implies a cost-effectiveness figure of $1503 per prevented smoker. If these adolescents do not go on to smoke at a later date, school prevention with media support is probably cost-effective, given the large health benefits which will accrue to them. However, since there is serious doubt about the long-term preventive effectiveness of such prevention programmes (Reid *et al.*, 1994) such a conclusion is tentative only.

5. Conclusion

It is frustrating that despite the abundance of media smoking evaluations none has been specifically designed with an economic evaluation component. Many simplifying assumptions have to be made in order to generate retrospective cost-effectiveness estimates from published studies. This inevitably makes such retrospective economic evaluation fragile. Nevertheless, it is worth while to gain approximate figures for the cost-effectiveness of different media interventions and as a guide to some of the possibilities and pitfalls involved in cost-effectiveness analysis. Table 4.4 summarises the results that have been discussed and derived in this chapter.

The cost-effectiveness of No Smoking Day has been addressed by several authors and, although estimation has been rough and ready, a cost of somewhere between £3 and £200 per life year saved seems plausible. Reid and Smith (1991) also present figures for a hypothetical national mass-media campaign at £4 per life year. Most other results have been based on American studies and so are less relevant to the UK. The Stanford Five Cities project appears to be relatively cost-effective at $35–$40 per quitter although these results are based on the cohort survey. The programme would not be judged cost-effective if judged on the cross-sectional results. Similarly the study by Danaher *et al.* (1984) of cessation kits finds they are less cost-effective if natural quit rates are taken into account.

In conclusion, it is not clear which mass-media interventions are most cost-effective. However, in general they seem to be about as cost-effective as brief GP advice and possibly more cost-effective than more intensive GP interventions. Chapter 5 uses some of the effectiveness evidence from this chapter, Chapter 2 and related appendices to test this hypothesis further.

Table 4.4: Summary of cost-effectiveness of mass-media campaigns

Type of campaign	Source study	Whose results?	Price year	Discount rate	Follow-up period (months)	Cost per quitter	Cost per life year (£)
No Smoking Day	Townsend (1986)	Townsend (1986)	1985	none applied	12		199
No Smoking Day	Reid and Smith (1991)	Reid and Smith (1991)	1989	none applied	12		3
No Smoking Day	Reid and Smith (1991)	This report	1989	none applied	12		15
National mass media	Reid and Smith (1991)	Reid and Smith (1991)	not clear	none applied	3		4
Community programme	Farquhar et al. (1990)	This report	not clear	none applied	17–60	$35–$40	
Cessation kit	NOP Market Research (1985a,b,c)	Flay (1987a)	not clear	none applied	3	£3.50	
Cessation kit	NOP Market Research (1985a,b,c)	This report	not clear	none applied	3		300
Cessation kit	Altman et al. (1987)	Altman et al. (1987)	1981	5% annually	5 weeks	$22–$144	
Cessation kit	Altman et al. (1987)	This report	1981	5% annually	5 weeks	$108–$721	
TV clinic	Best (1980)	Best (1980)	not clear	none applied	6	$48	
TV clinic	Danaher et al. (1984)	Danaher et al. (1984)	not clear	none applied	12	$27	
TV clinic	Danaher et al. (1984)	This report	not clear	none applied	12	$1503	
School prevention[1]	Flynn et al. (1992)	This report	not clear	none applied	12	$656–$1351	

[1]Figures for cost per prevented smoker

5. *POTENTIAL COST-EFFECTIVE SMOKING CESSATION INTERVENTIONS: AN EVALUATION OF TEN SCENARIOS*

Summary

- Effectiveness evidence from Chapters 2 to 4 is used to predict the quit rates associated with ten hypothetical interventions. A computer model, PREVENT, simulates the *final health gains* associated with the interventions.

- The costs of each intervention are estimated from the perspective of: the GP; the NHS; the smoker; and society. This allows comparable cost-effectiveness ratios to be constructed and a ranking of the interventions on cost-effectiveness grounds.

- The simulations are based on the presumption that all interventions will be successfully implemented and complied with nationwide. This is a simplification; the effects of low compliance are assessed. In general it will reduce the impact and cost-effectiveness of more intensive interventions.

- In conclusion, brief advice from a GP and No Smoking Day stand out as cost-effective and achievable smoking cessation interventions. Both have high impact, reaching a large number of smokers at low cost, £50–£350 per averted mortality from an NHS perspective, at zero discount rate. Antenatal smoking advice should also be a priority. More smokers can also be helped to quit successfully by the selective, properly targeted use of more intensive face-to-face and media interventions, where appropriate.

1. Introduction

Chapters 2 to 4 have shown that there is very little existing evidence on the cost-effectiveness of smoking cessation interventions. This is an obvious and serious gap in existing research. Much cost-effectiveness evidence that does exist derives from American sources published during the last decade. One approach to increase the usefulness of that information is simply to convert cost-effectiveness ratios to UK currency using national exchange rates or medical-specific purchasing power parities. However, conversion can lead to misleading results because the structure of health care systems is so diverse across countries. Considerable care should be taken in extrapolating the results from one country to another (Mason *et al.* 1993).

The main purpose of this chapter is therefore to develop tentative UK specific cost-effectiveness indicators for a number of interventions based on those from the review chapters and the studies referenced in Appendix B. The computer model PREVENT is used to simulate final health gains and cost estimates are developed for each intervention in turn. These are no substitute for more comprehensive and reliable economic evaluations. However, they may be of some use in framing research priorities and guiding local and national purchasers in their purchasing of smoking cessation health promotion.

The chapter is organised as follows. In section 2 the effectiveness evidence is summarised whilst section 3 introduces the PREVENT model. Quit rates are converted into expected final health gains in section 4 and cost estimation is also considered in section 5. Main results are presented in sections 6 and 7 where the effectiveness and cost data are combined to derive best and worst case cost-effectiveness indicators. The implications of these results are discussed in section 8 along with limitations and possible caveats. Some conclusions are given in section 9.

2. Effectiveness evidence

The quality and methodology of smoking cessation research does not enable many unequivocal conclusions to be made about effectiveness (see Appendix A). Despite this it is plain that brief advice from a GP can be an effective means of cessation. Effectiveness is enhanced by follow-up, more intensive counselling, commitment to quitting and aids such as nicotine gum and patches. Mass-media based approaches to cessation can also be effective and it is clear that more intensive approaches result in higher rates of long-term quitting. However, it is less obvious which are the most cost-effective interventions because costs are seldom reported in these studies and when they are a single aggregated figure is usually given. In consequence the cost estimates for media-based programmes in section 5 are speculative and likely to be less reliable than similar estimates for face-to-face interventions. Table 5.1 presents plausible 12-month baseline quit rates for ten major classes of intervention.

Chapters 2 to 4 and Appendix A also allow an indication of the likely range of quit rates associated with different interventions. Studies which have presented results at one year follow-up are included since this is the most common in the literature and because relapse is less likely. However, studies of transdermal nicotine patches (TNPs) and media campaigns tend to use shorter follow-up periods. Where this is the case subjective judgement is used in extrapo-lating to 12-month quit rates. The size of the sensitivity ranges in Table 5.1 reflects two processes. First, some interventions are broader than others. Consequently a wider range of quit rates is found in the literature, for example some highly intensive multiple intervention studies have pro-duced 12-month quit rates as high as 35 per cent. Second, they reflect the uncertainty associated with similar studies carried out in different countries or at different times. For example, several follow-up surveys of national No Smoking Days have found long-term quit rates varying between 0.1 and 0.5 per cent.

Table 5.1: Effectiveness of smoking cessation interventions

	Plausible one year net quit rates	
	Baseline (%)	*Sensitivity range (%)*
1. Brief advice or counselling from GP	5	3–10
2. GP advice plus nicotine gum	10	5–20
3. Brief advice plus other intervention(s) from GP	15	5–35
4. Advise patients to purchase TNPs	10	5–15
5. Advice in antenatal clinics to pregnant women	15	5–25
6. Information campaigns	4	0–10
7. No Smoking Day	0.3	0.1–0.5
8. TV cessation clinic	4	1–9
9. Community-wide TV campaign	5	3–10
10. Media promotion of cessation kits	6	1–15

Source: based on Chapters 2 to 4 and Appendix B.

The values from Table 5.1 are used as inputs into the PREVENT model which predicts the likely final health outcomes associated with smoking cessation.

3. The PREVENT model: converting quit rates to final health outcomes

The PREVENT model allows a sophisticated simulation of the health benefits arising from reductions in smoking prevalence. This is extremely useful when comparing the effectiveness and cost-effectiveness of cessation interventions with other forms of health promotion and health care. A detailed explanation of how the model works has been published elsewhere (Gunning-Schepers, 1989).

Much of PREVENT is based on conventional epidemiology. However, most epidemiological modelling is static; the innovation of PREVENT is that it is dynamic. In particular: a time dimension is included to simulate the gradual reduction in excess risk after exposure to smoking; a time factor is also introduced to control for the interaction between the effects of an intervention and predicted future demographic changes; and PREVENT takes account of the fact that smoking affects several diseases. This has important implications for predicted health benefits: health benefits will be delayed because ex-smokers are not assumed to return to the risk profiles of never-smokers; results will be different because of the inclusion of demographic trends; and overall estimates of health gain are likely to be higher than for simpler models because smoking is associated with several diseases.*

All simulations refer to the effects of a single intervention which takes place at the beginning of 1993 and results in one-year quit rates as detailed in Table 5.1. Several simplifying assumptions are also made. First, any intervention will reduce smoking prevalence equally across different age and sex bands. This may not be the case in reality if cohort effects dominate or interventions are targeted. Second, the impact of interventions is assumed continuous in PREVENT. An intervention which reduces smoking prevalence by 5 per cent over 12 months will continue to have an impact on younger cohorts as they enter the model. Smoking prevalence is considered permanently reduced. Smoking cessation interventions therefore result in similar 'prevention rates'. Whilst this may be a possible direct outcome from an intervention it is unlikely. However, there may be indirect avenues for prevention from a cessation campaign. Parental smoking is an important factor in teenage experimentation with cigarettes and if the result of an intervention is for parents to quit this may also lower smoking among children and teenagers. Interventions may also lower the overall level of smoking by social diffusion, especially in younger cohorts (Rosén and Lindholm, 1992). Nevertheless PREVENT will probably tend to overestimate the gains from cessation to some degree and this should be borne in mind.

Tables 5.2 and 5.3 show cumulative gains in health benefits accruing to the English and Welsh populations as a result of the one-year interventions given in Table 5.1. It is assumed that *every smoker* in the population is exposed to the intervention. This is unrealistic in most cases. Section 8 discusses the important issues associated with compliance and implementation. Intervention 5, advice to pregnant smokers in antenatal clinics, is an important omission from the following tables and discussion. It is not possible to include this intervention in the PREVENT model because it does not simulate health gains accruing to others apart from the smoker. Nevertheless, given the evidence from Chapter 3 it is clear that such advice should be given to all pregnant smokers.

The baseline quit rates and sensitivity ranges from Table 5.1 are linked to two final outcome measures using PREVENT: total mortality reduction (TMR) and actual life years gained (ALYG). TMR is simply the model's prediction of the impact of smoking cessation on the total number of deaths in England and Wales. ALYG is slightly more

---

*For example, Williams (1987) only calculates the gains from a reduction in the incidence of myocardial infarction and angina.

Table 5.2: The health benefits of cessation – baseline and sensitivity range estimates

Alternative scenarios	Health benefits to 2029			
	Total Mortality Reduction (TMR)		Actual life years gained (AYLG)	
	Baseline estimates	Sensitivity range	Baseline estimates	Sensitivity range
1. Brief advice from GP	53 789	42 754–81 495	902 527	652 226–1 529 954
2. GP advice plus nicotine gum	81 495	53 789–137 488	1 529 954	902 527–2 792 016
3. GP advice plus other intervention(s)	109 381	53 789–222 768	2 159 778	902 527–4 703 387
4. GP advises smokers to purchase TNPs	81 495	53 789–109 381	1 529 954	902 527–2 159 778
5. Advice or more for pregnant smokers	n.e.	n.e.	n.e.	n.e
6. Information campaigns	48 268	0–81,495	777 328	0–1 529 954
7. No Smoking Day[1]	9 526	3 175–15 877	120 690	40 230–201 151
8. TV cessation clinics	48 268	31 754–75 936	777 328	402 301–1 404 277
9. Community-wide TV campaign	53 789	42 754–81 495	902 527	635 226–1 529 954
10. Media promotion of cessation kits	59 311	31 754–109 381	1 027 826	402 301–2 159 778

[1] PREVENT only accepts integer values for interventions which reduce smoking prevalence. Our baseline quit rate for NSD is 0.3 per cent and sensitivity range 0.1 per cent to 0.5 per cent. We have assumed that the health benefits will be 30 per cent, and 10 per cent to 50 per cent of the benefits from an intervention which results in a 12-month quit rate of 1 per cent.

n.e: not estimated for this scenario.

Table 5.3: The health benefits of cessation – baseline and sensitivity range estimates at 6 per cent discount rate

Alternative scenarios

	Health benefits to 2029			
	Total mortality reduction (TMR)		Actual life years gained (AYLG)	
	Baseline estimates	Sensitivity range	Baseline estimates	Sensitivity range
1. Brief advice from GP	18 974	13 912–31 663	221 235	155 462–386 010
2. GP advice plus nicotine gum	31 633	18 974–57 188	386 010	221 235–717 029
3. GP advice plus other intervention(s)	44 402	18 974–95 852	551 274	221 235–1 160 227
4. GP advises smokers to purchase TNPs	31 663	18 974–44 402	386 010	221 235–551 274
5. Advice or more for pregnant smokers	n.e.	n.e.	n.e.	n.e.
6. Information campaigns	16 442	0–31 663	188 339	0–386 010
7. No Smoking Day[1]	2 658	886–4 430	26 930	8 977–44 883
8. TV cessation clinics	16 442	8 859–29 199	188 339	89 765–353 016
9. Community-wide TV campaign	18 974	13 912–31 663	221 235	155 462–386 010
10. Media promotion of cessation kits	21 506	8 859–44 402	254 153	89 765–551 274

[1] PREVENT only accepts integer values for interventions which reduce smoking prevalence. Our baseline quit rate for NSD is 0.3 per cent and sensitivity range 0.1 per cent to 0.5 per cent. We have assumed that the health benefits will be 30 per cent, and 10 per cent to 50 per cent of the benefits from an intervention which results in a 12-month quit rate of 1 per cent.

n.e: not estimated for this scenario

complicated and measures the predicted cumulative additional years of life due to smoking cessation.

4. The health benefits of smoking cessation

Table 5.2 shows that 12 months of consistent brief advice dispensed opportunistically from GPs to all smoking patients is predicted to result in 54 000 averted deaths and 900 000 actual life years gained to the year 2029. Other interventions, especially highly intensive multiple interventions from GPs, could avoid even more premature deaths. Table 5.2 also details the range of expected final health gains associated with the sensitivity ranges in Table 5.1.

Table 5.3 reports the health benefits of the various interventions discounted at 6 per cent per annum* to 2029 (see Chapter 1 for a discussion of discounting). Discounting has a significant effect on the magnitude of expected total health gains, reducing them by between 200 and 400 per cent. It also has important implications for the cost-effectiveness of health promotion and prevention activities *versus* treatment or cure options. Most costs are incurred immediately (for example No Smoking Day) and remain undiscounted. In contrast benefits are delayed and are heavily discounted. Prevention therefore suffers in cost-effectiveness comparisons because the benefits from treatment or cure options tend to occur in a shorter timescale and thus are discounted less. The validity of discounting health benefits is a controversial issue amongst health economists. Parsonage and Neuberger (1992) argue that benefits should remain undiscounted, partly on the grounds that health promotion and education options will therefore be more attractive investments.† Consequently, results are reported for both zero and 6 per cent discounted rates throughout this chapter.

5. Costs of reaching smokers with the interventions

Each intervention considered in Table 5.1 costs money to implement. Because of the hypothetical nature of this exercise costs need to be estimated. Constructing cost estimates from first principles unavoidably entails uncertainty and many assumptions and problems. Inevitably some relevant cost categories are not available. The purpose of Table C.1 in Appendix C is to show exactly what is included in the cost figures given in Table 5.4. Appendix C also gives in-depth details of the collection and estimation of costs themselves with sources and assumptions regarding baseline and sensitivity ranges.

The figures in Table 5.4 have been calculated in two ways. The cost of interventions 1 to 4 has been calculated on a per smoker basis. These costs have been multiplied by 11 914 400, the estimated number of total

---

*The present UK Treasury discount rate for discounting public projects.

†The Department of Health and the Treasury appear to have agreed to a change in procedure regarding discounting and the evaluation of health-care projects (Parsonage and Neuberger, 1991).

Table 5.4: Costs of smoking interventions

Alternative scenarios

	Range of plausible 1993 cost estimates (£)			
	GP	Additional costs to NHS/sponsor	Smoker	Society
1. Brief advice from GP	4 467 900–14 773 856	None	1 036 553	5 504 453–15 810 409
2. GP advice plus nicotine gum	13 403 700–44 321 568	None	326 943 051–434 887 515	371 264 619–448 291 215
3. GP advice plus other intervention(s)	162 691 132–442 739 104	23 828 800	48 855 712	235 375 644–515 423 616
4. GP advises smokers to purchase TNPs	13 403 700–44 321 568	None	442 241 957–690 910 999	486 563 525–704 313 799
5. Advice or more for pregnant smokers	n.e.	n.e.	n.e.	n.e.
6. Information campaigns	n.a.	5 000 000	?	?
7. No Smoking Day	n.a.	1 000 000	?	?
8. TV cessation clinics	n.a.	20 000	?	?
9. Community-wide TV campaign	?	10 000 000	?	20 000 000
10. Media promotion of cessation kits	n.a.	1 000 000	?	?

?: reliable estimation problematical

n.a.: not applicable to this scenario

n.e.: not estimated

smokers in England and Wales in 1993.★ In contrast the cost of scenarios 6 to 10 have been estimated directly from details on total expenditure for various campaigns in the literature and from the Health Education Authority.

Costs are also estimated from a variety of different perspectives. The perspectives considered are the most obvious and useful to purchasers, they are the perspective of the GP, the NHS or local sponsoring health or voluntary agencies, the exposed smoker and society. The costs to the GP comprise the opportunity cost of their time, overheads and administration. In most cases there are assumed to be no additional costs to the NHS, although printed materials are included in scenario 4. The costs to the smoker comprise the opportunity cost of time, travel and predicted costs of a course of nicotine gum or patches under scenarios 2 and 4. The costs to society are defined as the sum of the costs to the GP, NHS and the smoker. Data on mass-media campaigns come from a variety of sources. Unfortunately there are not enough reliable data to estimate costs from the perspective of the smoker for mass-media campaigns (see Appendix C for details).

The most expensive scenarios from society's perspective are intensive face-to-face interventions, costing anything from £235 million to £704 million per annum. Most of this cost is borne by the smoker. In comparison the mass-media campaigns are far cheaper, most of the cost being borne by the sponsor. However, the intensive face-to-face interventions also have the greatest potential health impact (see Tables 5.2 and 5.3). Sections 6 and 7 discuss whether they are cost-effective.

6. Cost-effectiveness ratios under worst and best cases at zero discount rate

Tables 5.5 and 5.6 illustrate the estimated cost-effectiveness, in terms of cost per averted mortality and cost per life year gained respectively, of the various options at a zero per cent discount rate. Best and worst case scenarios are constructed to show the best and worst possible cost-effectiveness of each intervention, given our assumptions. The best (worst) case is derived from dividing the least (most) expensive estimate of possible costs for each scenario from Table 5.4 and dividing it by the highest (lowest) health gain figures for that scenario from the PREVENT simulations in Table 5.2.

It is clear that brief advice alone from a GP is likely to be the most cost-effective of the face-to-face interventions, costing £67–£370 per averted mortality and £3–£24 per life year gained, from a societal perspective depending on assumptions. This arises because it takes much less time on behalf of both patient and GP – opportunity costs are therefore low. Although multiple interventions can be the most effective intervention by

★The number of smokers was estimated from data on prevalence from the *General Household Survey 1992* (OPCS, 1994) and from data on the size of the adult population from *Population Trends*. Interpolation was used to derive the 1993 estimate of 11.9 million.

Table 5.5: Cost per averted mortality – best and worst case at zero discount rate

Alternative scenarios

	Cost per averted mortality (£)			
	GP	NHS or sponsor	Smoker	Society
1. Brief advice from GP	54.83–345.55	n.a.	12.72–24.25	67.54–369.80
2. GP advice plus nicotine gum	97.49–823.99	n.a.	6 078.25–3 163.09	3 260.58–6 902.24
3. GP advice plus other intervention(s)	730.32–8 231.03	106.97–443.00	219.31–908.28	1 056.60–9 582.32
4. GP advises smokers to purchase TNPs	129.54–823.99	n.a.	6 316.55–8 221.79	6 439.09–9 045.78
5. Advice or more for pregnant smokers	n.e.	n.e.	n.e.	n.e.
6. Information campaigns	n.a.	61.35–∞	?	?
7. No Smoking Day	n.a.	62.98–314.48	?	?
8. TV cessation clinics	n.a.	0.26–0.63	?	?
9. Community-wide TV campaign	?	122.71–233.90	?	245.22+–467.80+
10. Media promotion of cessation kits	n.a.	9.14–31.49	?	?

?: reliable estimation problematical

n.a.: not applicable to this scenario

n.e.: not estimated

Table 5.6: Cost per life year gained – best and worst case at zero discount rate

Alternative scenarios	Cost per life year gained (£)			
	GP	NHS or sponsor	Smoker	Society
1. Brief advice from GP	2.92–22.65	n.a.	0.68–1.59	3.60 – 24.24
2. GP advice plus nicotine gum	4.80–49.11	n.a.	155.76 – 362.25	160.56–411.36
3. GP advice plus other intervention(s)	34.59–490.55	5.07–26.40	10.39–54.13	50.04–571.09
4. GP advises smokers to purchase TNPs	6.21–49.11	n.a.	319.90–490.00	326.10–539.11
5. Advice or more for pregnant smokers	n.e.	n.e.	n.e.	n.e.
6. Information campaigns	n.a.	3.27–∞	?	?
7. No Smoking Day	n.a.	4.98–24.86	?	?
8. TV cessation clinics	n.a.	0.01–0.05	?	?
9. Community-wide TV campaign	?	6.54–15.31	?	13.08+–30.62+
10. Media promotion of cessation kits	n.a.	0.46–2.49	?	?

?: reliable estimation problematical
n.a.: not applicable to this scenario
n.e.: not estimated

a long way they are also very costly for both smokers and GPs, costing £1 050–£9 580 per averted mortality and £50–£570 per life year gained.

Brief advice alone is also likely to be more cost-effective than brief advice plus nicotine gum or TNPs. Although from the NHS perspective these are more cost-effective than multiple interventions they are the least cost-effective from the smoker's perspective. Because the cost of the interventions falls almost exclusively on the smoker this will lead to serious compliance problems (see section 8). TNPs are less cost-effective than nicotine gum in our tables. This arises because they are more expensive, and because we assume they are less effective at 12 months, this assumption may need to be modified in the light of forthcoming TNP trial results.

The fact that media interventions seem more cost-effective from the NHS/sponsor perspective should not be taken to imply that they are also more cost-effective from the smokers' or societal perspectives. There is simply too little information to make a judgement. The estimates of cost-effectiveness should therefore be treated very cautiously. In fact, as can be seen from Tables 5.5 and 5.6, so little information was available that some estimates are not presented.

The costs and health benefits associated with scenarios 6 to 10 are not known with any confidence. The most reliable mass-media estimate is that connected with No Smoking Day. For this scenario both the costs (incurred by the HEA) and effectiveness (evaluated by several others) are known with some confidence. Although this event is much less effective than many other possible interventions it is also much cheaper and leads to substantial numbers of quitters even at 12-months follow-up, resulting in cost-effectiveness ratios of £63–£315 per averted mortality and £5–£25 per life year saved, from a sponsor's perspective. The costs incurred by local and voluntary agencies on No Smoking Day are likely to be understated. These need to be properly measured and tallied if society's costs are not to be underestimated.

Finally, comparing options 1 and 7 it can be seen that No Smoking Day is broadly as cost-effective as receiving brief advice from a GP.

7. Cost-effectiveness ratios under worst and best cases at 6 per cent discount rate

Discounting health benefits has a large effect on the cost-effectiveness of any health promotion interventions since most of the health benefits only become apparent in the future (see Chapter 1). This can be seen by looking at Tables 5.7 and 5.8. Discounting has the effect of making all options less cost-effective versus other health care interventions since the benefits from treatment are more immediate. This is important when comparing the desirability of smoking cessation policy versus wider health care policy options. However, it has no effect on the rankings of the interventions.

Table 5.7: Cost per averted mortality – best and worst case at 6% discount rate

Alternative scenarios	*Cost per averted mortality (£)*			
	GP	*NHS*	*Smoker*	*Society*
1. Brief advice from GP	141.11–1 061.95	n.a.	32.74–74.51	173.85–1 136.46
2. GP advice plus nicotine gum	234.38–2 335.91	n.a.	7 604.52–17 231.11	7 838.90–19 567.02
3. GP advice plus other intervention(s)	1 697.32–23 333.99	248.60–1 519.38	509.70–2 574.88	2 455.61–27 184.73
4. GP advises smokers to purchase TNPs	301.87–2 335.91	n.a.	15 560.36–23 307.79	15 862.21–25 643.70
5. Advice or more for pregnant smokers	n.e.	n.e.	n.e.	n.e.
6. Information campaigns	n.a.	157.91–∞	?	?
7. No Smoking Day	n.a.	225.74–1 128.66	?	?
8. TV cessation clinics	n.a.	0.69–2.26	?	?
9. Community-wide TV campaign	?	315.83–718.60	?	631.65+ – 1 437.61+
10. Media promotion of cessation kits	n.a.	22.52–112.88	?	?

?: reliable estimation problematical
n.a.: not applicable to this scenario
n.e.: not estimated

Table 5.8: Cost per life year saved – best and worst case at 6% discount rate

Alternative scenarios	Cost per life year saved (£)			
	GP	*NHS*	*Smoker*	*Society*
1. Brief advice from GP	11.57–95.03	n.a.	2.69–6.67	14.26–101.70
2. GP advice plus nicotine gum	18.69–200.34	n.a.	606.51–1 447.81	625.21–1 648.15
3. GP advice plus other intervention(s)	140.22–2001.22	20.54–107.71	42.11–2 20.84	202.87–2 329.76
4. GP advises smokers to purchase TNPs	24.31–200.34	n.a.	1 235.30–1 998.97	1 227.61–2 199.31
5. Advice or more for pregnant smokers	n.e.	n.e.	n.e.	n.e.
6. Information campaigns	n.a.	12.95–∞	?	?
7. No Smoking Day	n.a.	22.28–111.40	?	?
8. TV cessation clinics	n.a.	0.06–0.22	?	?
9. Community-wide TV campaign	?	25.91–64.32	?	51.81+– 128.65+
10. Media promotion of cessation kits	n.a.	1.81–11.14	?	?

?: reliable estimation problematical

n.a.: not applicable to this scenario

n.e.: not estimated

The health benefits, costs and cost-effectiveness indicators generated in this chapter have been hypothetical only. They are based on the assumption of the *full participation of all smokers* in England and Wales. In practice the health benefits may be overestimated and the cost estimates underestimated. Use of sensitivity analysis and worst and best case scenarios compensates for these problems to some degree. This section discusses the limitations of the simulation approach and implications for cost-effectiveness in practice.

Implementation

Implementation is a key issue. It relates to the delivery or supply of smoking cessation interventions to the patient. Tables 5.3 and 5.4 report the simulated health gains to 2029 if *all* smokers in England and Wales are exposed to the intervention in question. This is because PREVENT simulates health gains for whole populations. In the case of mass-media based interventions this means that all smokers see the televised commercials or programmes, read the newspapers or receive the leaflets. For face-to-face interventions it implies that all smokers see their GP and, where appropriate, receive a private prescription for nicotine gum or TNPs and return for follow-up appointments.

In reality not all smokers will be exposed to the interventions. This is a simplifying assumption, and the results in Tables 5.2 and 5.3 should therefore be viewed as the *maximum* potential health benefits arising from each scenario. In reality the gain in averted mortality will be lower although no allowance was made in the simulations for other health benefits. The recent government initiatives on health promotion in general practice are encouraging but they demonstrate the financial burden involved in ensuring that GPs at least monitor smoking and other risk factor behaviour.★ There is no guarantee that GPs will consistently offer even brief smoking cessation advice to smokers. More intensive interventions and those which rely on prescriptions for cessation products such as gum and TNPs would in practice be harder to implement widely (see Chapter 2).

This has different consequences for the cost-effectiveness of face-to-face and population interventions. Since the face-to-face scenarios have been calculated on a per-smoker basis less than 100 per cent implementation has no effect on the cost-effectiveness indicators since the costs of the intervention for smokers that do not receive them are not

---

★The health promotion bandings scheme is forecast to cost around £80 million in registration payments alone in 1993–94. In many instances this simply secures monitoring of patients' smoking status and other CVD risk factors. This does not include the costs of actually administering interventions.

incurred.★ In contrast the mass-media based cost estimates are based on one-off costs associated with a campaign. If less than 100 per cent of smokers receive the intervention this will reduce the projected health benefits but not the costs. The cost-effectiveness ratios of mass-media interventions in this chapter may therefore be overestimated relative to face-to-face interventions.

Compliance

Compliance is also a key issue. It relates to the demand for, or uptake of, cessation interventions by the smoker. Even if there are no problems with the supply or implementation of interventions compliance difficulties will have major implications for the effectiveness and cost-effectiveness of the hypothetical interventions in practice. The fact that PREVENT assumes population coverage is obviously an over-simplification. A large minority of smokers in the population will not be motivated or willing to quit smoking. Interventions in this group will be far less effective than in the majority. The impact of population-based interventions may therefore be less than small-scale trials indicate.

Compliance problems are also likely to be more severe with face-to-face interventions than in media-based approaches. This is because many media interventions are passive in the first instance, and information can be readily absorbed and obtained at little cost to the individual. In contrast face-to-face interventions require some physical action in the first instance and in the case of nicotine gum and TNPs, a large financial outlay.

However, a brief intervention consisting of anti-smoking advice during an existing consultation is likely to maximise compliance and thus impact. Eighty per cent of the UK population see their GP annually (Fry, 1993) and there is evidence to suggest that smokers consult their GP more often than non-smokers (Godfrey *et al.*, 1993). The majority of smokers are therefore currently in a position to be opportunistically counselled, however briefly, to quit or reduce their consumption.

For other face-to-face interventions however, high compliance is much less likely. Multiple interventions require dedicated and therefore previously arranged consultations. Aggregate health benefits from this option are therefore likely to be dramatically overestimated by PREVENT simply because the majority of smokers would not attend appointments. On the other hand those who are willing to take part are more likely to be motivated to quit; costs will also be reduced since fewer consultations and materials will be consumed. A multiple intervention approach may be

---

★The exception to this is if the fixed costs of the health promotion banding fees are included in the cost figures for the GP-based scenarios. We have omitted them in this analysis because of the difficulty of apportioning resource use to smoking cessation and other health promotion interventions. It will also have an effect on impact since the health benefits in Tables 5.2 and 5.3 are based on the assumption of all smokers receiving interventions.

cost-effective for certain groups, if the costs of initially contacting smokers can be kept low. Its impact will, however, be low.

Similarly, most of the nicotine gum and TNP studies reviewed in Chapter 2 are controlled trials which compared treatment and non-treatment groups. Reported quit-rates therefore pertain to a group of smokers with 100 per cent compliance. This is highly unlikely in a non-experimental setting. Oster *et al.* (1986) assume a 25 per cent compliance rate and even this may be optimistic (Saul, 1993). In practice the health benefits flowing from options 2 and 4 will be less than reported in Tables 5.2 and 5.3. Cost-effectiveness will only suffer if gum and TNPS are purchased but unused. As it is, Tables 5.5 to 5.8 suggest that gum and TNPs are not cost-effective compared to advice alone.

Compliance with media-based programmes relies less on the smoker in the first instance and more on the costs involved with marketing. Mass media, and particularly television, are uniquely powerful in being able to reach a wide audience very quickly (Reid *et al.*, 1992). Compliance, to delivery of the message at least, is almost guaranteed since commercials can be aired at prime-time to maximise audience ratings figures.

Mass-media advertising can also be used for targeting, if enough is known about the age, sex and socio-economic characteristics of viewers on different days at different times. TV cessation programmes attempt to recreate the inter-personal effect of face-to-face interventions by following the cessation experiences of other smokers or well-known personalities. However, although long-term compliance may be greater amongst the audience, the audience itself will be much smaller than with a paid advertising campaign. The final health outcomes and impact of TV cessation programmes are therefore overestimated in Tables 5.5 to 5.8. Because of the fixed costs of production and broadcasting cost-effectiveness will also be overestimated. Similar arguments hold for promotion of cessation kits.

Finally No Smoking Days have been extensively evaluated. Awareness is extremely high, McGuire (1992) calculates that over 90 per cent of British smokers are aware of No Smoking Day. Compliance is taken into account in the quit rate figures given in Table 5.1. Cost-effectiveness is therefore not altered by consideration of compliance problems. Although aimed at short-term cessation No Smoking Day is also effective in helping a small percentage of people to quit each year. It would become more cost-effective if the short-term health benefits accruing to temporary quitters were taken into account. The cost-effectiveness of other options is more speculative but it is unlikely that they would turn out to be less cost-effective than most face-to-face interventions.

Cost

Much of the economic evaluation literature concentrates on cost-effectiveness, and which interventions will return the highest effectiveness for least cost. However, at a national level the issue of total expenditure also becomes important. Because of the time and individual materials involved, face-to-face interventions are very costly in absolute terms. Table 5.4 shows that face-to-face interventions, which reach every smoker in England and Wales, could cost the NHS anything from £4.5 to £467 million in a single year. The total HEA budget is only of the order of £30 million per year of which around £5 million is spent on anti-smoking education. At a local level brief advice alone (£4.5 to £14.8 million nationally) could possibly be implemented. Any successful blanket implementation of intensive face-to-face interventions nationwide will require a major political decision within the Department of Health.

Reduced effectiveness of repeated interventions

Another concern in the longer run is the possibility of reduced effectiveness and therefore cost-effectiveness through time. The first year of a widescale and successful intervention could lead to quit rates similar to those reported in Table 5.1. However, interventions in further years will not be as successful simply because the most motivated and least addicted smokers are more likely to quit in the first year. Over time the remaining core of smokers may become more difficult to reach and help with brief simple interventions.★ This raises the possibility that the greater use of targeted, intensive interventions will become more cost-effective as smoking rates decline. A continuing assessment of the cost-effectiveness of targeted versus population approaches to smoking cessation is crucial if valuable resources are to be spent wisely.

9. Summary and conclusion

The potential for intensive face-to-face interventions to deliver health gains is significantly reduced once problems of compliance and implementation are taken into account. It is doubtful whether large scale implementation therefore offers a cost-effective or sensible use of resources at present. Selectively targeting these interventions at individuals who experience greater difficulty with cessation is likely to be more rational. This in turn implies more research into the mechanisms of smoking cessation.

Media programmes are much easier to implement in general as they do not rely on the motivation of thousands of GPs but a much smaller group of personnel in health organisations around the country. However, where community involvement is high correct implementation can become complex and possible costly. Nevertheless implementation issues are much less of a constraint than with face-to-face interventions. Media approaches also tend to cost far less than face-to-face interventions. Although the opportunity cost of smokers' time and that of society are ignored in the tables above, from an NHS or sponsor's perspective media-based

---

★One way to test this proposition is to investigate the effectiveness results in non-volunteer trials of smoking cessation over time.

interventions appear much more cost-effective than most face-to-face alternatives. One expensive media intervention can reach thousands or millions of smokers at a time, whereas face-to-face interventions can become hugely expensive when aggregated and have poor impact once compliance and implementation are taken into account.

Two of the ten interventions are particularly attractive on cost-effectiveness and other grounds:

- Brief advice from a GP, as part of an existing consultation, is the only face-to-face intervention which appears to be cost-effective and robust to issues of compliance, implementation and budget constraints.
- Similarly No Smoking Day is proven to reach the majority of smokers at low overall cost and with high cost-effectiveness.

These at present offer the best value for money smoking cessation interventions but they also appear to be two of the least effective options analysed. However, this is partly illusory, since the effectiveness of other face-to-face interventions is reduced once compliance and implementation are addressed. Other media programmes have the potential to be more effective but they have not been reliably evaluated or costed in a UK setting and remain as yet unproven. This is an urgent area for research. It is also clear, from Chapter 3, that antenatal smoking advice to all pregnant smokers is a worthwhile exercise on health and financial grounds.

There is clearly a need to fill the obvious gaps and inadequacies in existing research. This chapter has attempted a very tentative economic evaluation of several smoking cessation interventions. Although there are good studies of smoking cessation, generalisability and comparability are usually poor and cost information virtually non-existent. Despite the great advances in knowledge of the harm that tobacco causes there is still remarkably little information on how a successful smoking cessation intervention can be reliably and cost-effectively implemented.

In the short term two possible options exist in order to improve effectiveness and impact. First, GPs could easily disseminate self-help materials to their existing smokers as and when they arrive for an existing consultation. Appendix C shows that such material can be an exceptionally cheap method of reminding and helping about cessation. Secondly, the emphasis of No Smoking Day could usefully be extended into the area of long-term abstinence, indeed over 40 per cent of smokers already perceive its main purpose to be to encourage smokers to quit for good (McGuire, 1992). More smokers can also be reached and helped to quit successfully by selective, properly targeted use of other face-to-face and mass-media interventions where appropriate.

APPENDICES

Appendix A *Evaluation of smoking cessation studies: problems and issues*

<u>*1. Introduction*</u>

The purpose of this appendix is to outline the problems that arise in the evaluation of smoking cessation studies and to give guidelines on the critical assessment of available research. An economic framework is a useful starting point both to guide prospective evaluations and to classify where problems with individual existing studies may arise. There are seven distinct stages in a basic economic evaluation: problem definition; setting of economic objectives; choice of options for appraisal; study design; collection of cost data; collection of outcome data; and generation of cost-effectiveness ratios. This evaluation framework is also valid for assessing evaluations without an economic component. In this case there are fewer stages: problem definition; medical objectives; choice of options; study design; and collection of outcome data. If severe methodological or practical problems arise at any one of these steps study results may be seriously compromised or invalidated.

External and internal validity are necessary if study results can be used to inform policy choices. Most internal validity problems arise due to deficiencies in study design which may make inference invalid and attribution of cause and effect uncertain. However, these study design problems are usually caused further up the chain. For example, ambiguities of problem definition may lead to poor study design through the omission of a relevant option. External validity is needed if results are to be generalised.

Tolley (1993) develops three summary criteria – scope, generalisability and comparability – which can be used to provide an overall assessment of the quality of findings from studies. The latter two address external validity. Generalisability concerns the wider relevance of the results of the study for practical implementation and policy. Comparability of findings across studies is important for determining reliability in order to rank alternative smoking cessation or prevention interventions according to their cost-effectiveness. Problems with internal validity obviously reduce external validity but internally valid studies may still be difficult to generalise or compare because of, for instance, non-standard techniques, different populations, unrealistic idealised study conditions and different costing structures and outcome measures.

Because the smoking cessation literature is so varied there are few standard methods or procedures, comparability and generalisability are inevitably compromised. In section 2 common problems which affect internal validity are reviewed. This section is structured according to the economic framework set out above. The problems that may arise with external validity independently of the internal validity of a paper are considered in section 3. Section 4 concludes.

2. Internal validity

Problem definition

The perspective adopted is a key determinant in the framing of problem definition in cost-effectiveness studies. In the health education context four levels of problem definition can be defined:

- Level 1. What is the cost-effectiveness of alternative health education interventions? For example, a district health authority may wish to explore the cost-effectiveness of providing leaflets about smoking at an antenatal clinic compared to employing a specialist to provide face-to-face counselling for the same group.
- Level 2. What is the cost-effectiveness of health education compared to alternative health promotion interventions? This could involve a comparison of all the alternative methods for reducing the consumption of tobacco and prevalence of smoking discussed in Chapter 1.
- Level 3. What is the cost-effectiveness of health education compared to treatment and curative interventions? For example this may involve a comparison of health education directed at smoking compared to the costs and benefits of treatments for smoking-related diseases.
- Level 4. What is the cost-effectiveness of health education compared to allocating additional resources to other public sector services? This is the broadest type of cost-effectiveness evaluation and would involve questions such as, for example, whether more should be spent on a smoking campaign or crime prevention.

The level of the analysis undertaken is determined by the perspective taken. For example, a narrow perspective would be that of a single-agency provider, such as a district health authority (DHA), workplace or the Health Education Authority (HEA), adopting a level 1 type evaluation. Higher levels require broader perspectives which are usually multi-agency in origin, for example an evaluation of a community smoking prevention programme could involve local DHAs, voluntary organisations, the media and the HEA. In this case costs incurred from all these perspectives need to be taken into account and measured if the true costs of the intervention are to be known.

The perspective taken is instrumental in determining the broad magnitude of costs incurred and the size of cost-effectiveness ratios generated. It is therefore crucial that:

- The perspective taken is either explicitly stated and explained or is implicitly clear from the content and argument of a paper.
- When comparing results from two or more studies the perspectives adopted in each study are identical or very similar.

The first condition ensures that cost–effectiveness results are set in some context. If the perspective is not known it is difficult to evaluate and subsequently replicate the study since it is not possible to check that all relevant costs have been measured. A number of cost–effectiveness studies fail on this point.

The first condition is also necessary but not sufficient to compare the results validly from different studies. Perspectives must not only be known but also be identical or very similar across the studies. If not, then misleading cost–effectiveness rankings and policy guidelines can result. Mason *et al.* (1993) raise this problem in a discussion of the wider use and abuse of cost–effectiveness league tables.

The study of McParlane *et al.* (1987) can be used to illustrate the significance of adopting different perspectives. McParlane and colleagues report the results of a quasi-experimental trial to market smoking and pregnancy education materials to physicians in Houston, Texas. A volunteer attempted to sell the kit to each practice visited. The perspectives adopted are stated explicitly as those of a voluntary health organisation (VHO) and society. The cost categories measured were: personnel; transport; supplies; physician and volunteer time; and materials. Their cost–effectiveness results are reproduced in the table below.

Table A.1: Effects on cost–effectiveness ratios of different perspectives

Perspective	Cost per visit ($)	Cost per purchase ($)
Single agency	16.36	30.55
Society	50.52	94.36

Source: McParlane *et al.* (1987)

Costs per visit or per purchase are half as much for a single agency as for society. Therefore the cost–effectiveness of the intervention from a single agency's perspective is twice as great as that from society's perspective. This difference arises because the costs of volunteer and physician time are only included in the calculation of society's costs, they are not incurred by the VHO.

In order to interpret cost–effectiveness ratios correctly the perspective must be known. Several authors reviewed in this report argue that smoking cessation interventions, based on their results, are more cost-effective than the pharmacologic treatment of mild hypertension and high cholesterol levels in middle-aged men. Whilst this may be true they allude only to headline cost-effectiveness figures and make no attempt to analyse or explain the perspectives adopted in these comparison studies. Such claims should therefore be treated cautiously.

Economic and health objectives

The economic and/or health objectives derived from the consideration of the study problem should relate directly to that problem. In general this aspect of internal validity is uncontroversial and it is fairly clear which are the health objectives of interest. These in turn can be readily converted to economic objectives, such as lowest cost per unit of outcome or greatest outcomes per unit of cost.

The main objective in the smoking cessation literature has been the increase in short- and long-term quit rates and reductions in the prevalence of cigarette smoking. Whether this is too restrictive is discussed in '(f) Outcomes' below.

Choice of options

All relevant options should be included in the study once problem definition and health and economic objectives have been decided. One of the most common and serious mistakes in both effectiveness and cost-effectiveness studies is the exclusion of a valid 'do-nothing' option. Health promotion interventions do not necessarily result in better health outcomes or positive changes in behaviour beyond that which would have occurred without the intervention. If this is not taken into account naturally occurring health behaviour or outcome changes may be mistakenly ascribed to the intervention. This is a particularly relevant concern in smoking cessation interventions since there is a long-term trend towards lower prevalence rates in all developed countries. Harris (1983) and Stoto (1986) have estimated an annual permanent but variable quit rate of 2-3 per cent amongst existing smokers due to self-help methods. This corresponds to one UK study of the determinants of smoking behaviour where a 3 per cent decline in tobacco consumption per year was ascribed to general health education activities (Godfrey and Maynard, 1988). In the absence of a 'do-nothing' control group authors should at least use available secondary information about population quit rates to assess the net effectiveness of their reported interventions. Only if interventions achieve quit rates significantly greater than this will they be effective and possibly cost-effective.

However, this issue can be more complex especially in face-to-face interventions such as advice or counselling supplied by GPs. Many, if not all, GPs routinely give smoking advice as part of standard practice therefore including a 'normal practice' control may be more desirable than a 'do-nothing' control. Since advice given as standard practice is likely to result in some additional quitting relative to doing nothing including only a 'do-

'nothing' control will overestimate the impact of a given intervention when it moves from being a trial to being executed more widely. This point is closely related to the problems of generalising trial results or of moving from ideal conditions to wider implementation. In order to be confident in the effectiveness results of a study it is important to assess whether it has included:

- A 'do-nothing' option or at least some discussion of secondary data on naturally occurring quit rates to assess the additional effectiveness of an intervention over simply leaving things as they are.
- A discussion of whether a control for 'normal practice' should also be included, instead of or as well as a 'do-nothing' option, since some minimal level of smoking cessation advice or other intervention is standard practice.

These considerations apply equally to population or mass-media approaches to smoking cessation and prevention. For example the organisers of a prospective media-led local community cessation campaign need to assess the current level of such health promotion activity and its relationship to local cessation in order properly to attribute additional behaviour change to the intervention.

The American television clinic study described by Danaher *et al.* (1984) suffered from the lack of a 'do-nothing' control. Evaluation was by means of two surveys. One found that 6.2 per cent of those who registered for materials associated with the campaign were continuously quit to 12 months. The second was a random telephone survey of local people who were smokers at the beginning of the campaign: 2.4 per cent were continuously abstinent to 12 months. The authors argue that 2.4 per cent of the local population of smokers or 72 000 quit due to the campaign plus 6.2 per cent of registrants, a further 217. Since the costs of the programme were stated as $200 000, cost per average quitter is $27. However, a later independent survey of smokers found that 2.9 per cent of the local population permanently quit each year independently of the state of media cessation interventions. In reality it is likely that 72 000 would have quit anyway regardless of the campaign and only 3.8 per cent of registrants would have been induced to quit as a direct result. This leaves only 133 quitters at a cost per average quitter of $1503.

Study design

The construction of a rigorous and reliable study design is critical to enable the attribution of specific behavioural and health outcomes to different interventions. Three broad types of study design are common: experimental; quasi-experimental; and non-experimental. Experimental designs are relatively common in face-to-face interventions and usually involve randomised control trials (RCTs) where participants are randomly assigned to intervention and control groups (of whatever nature). RCTs are well structured and consequently internal validity is usually high. A drawback is that the results are less generalisable to actual settings. Quasi-experimental designs overcome this problem by testing effectiveness of interventions in actual settings (for example through pre- and post-testing and matching intervention populations with controls). These studies are more generalisable and have higher external validity although it is more difficult to identify cause and effect due to confounding factors. Non-experimental studies are often used when it is infeasible or expensive to collect large amounts of data. In this case assumptions are drawn from the literature or prior epidemiological evidence.

An example of a non-experimental study is Oster *et al.* (1986) in which the cost-effectiveness of using nicotine gum as an adjunct to physician advice in a GP setting was assessed. The study concentrated on a hypothetical cohort of 250 patients who receive advice and a prescription for gum. Figures for the effectiveness of advice and advice plus gum were estimated from a literature review and linked to final health outcomes using epidemiological data. Costs associated with the intervention were also estimated from relevant sources. Internal validity is of course compromised but this is alleviated by the inclusion of a comprehensive sensitivity analysis. More specific problems are discussed below.

The most common consequence of non-ideal study design is that behavioural or health outcomes cannot be confidently attributed to the separate components of an intervention or the intervention as a whole. These are caused in the main by two characteristics of smoking cessation and smoking cessation studies:

- The psychological and addictive nature of smoking.
- Lack of adequate control for confounding factors and misattribution amongst the various components of an intervention.

Smoking cessation is troublesome to evaluate because of its inherent psychological nature. Although smokers can permanently quit due to a single, well-defined cause or event this is unlikely in practice. Smokers will quit for a variety of inter-related and reinforcing reasons and research has shown that most ex-smokers have passed through a cycle of temporary quitting and relapse episodes before final success which is related to the addictive nature of nicotine (Prochaska and DiClemente, 1983). Smokers who appear to have quit as a direct result of an intervention therefore have a history of previous quit attempts behind them. The cumulative effects of past smoking cessation campaigns and interventions is likely to be under estimated and mistakenly credited to the current intervention. However, the relative contribution of current and past interventions is almost impossible to differentiate in practice no matter the strength of a study design.

The other problems of confounding factors and misattribution are more amenable to control through the use of a good study design. These are closely related and arise in both face-to-face and population studies:

- Confounding factors refers to the existence of alternative, independent factors which could account for a study's findings.
- Misattribution refers to the assignment of outcomes to the wrong cause within a study design.

For example Doxiadis *et al.* (1985) report the results of a two-year television and radio anti-smoking campaign in Greece. Although there was a significant decline in smoking prevalence this could have been due to the confounding factor of a concurrent government imposed advertising ban. Similar problems arise when national campaigns are accompanied by independent campaigns at local level. Of course if prior knowledge existed this could be used to enhance the complexity of a study design with different intensities of activity in different areas. However, community programmes with many parallel events and activities can still make attribution of cause and effect complicated.

Misattribution is probably more common than the existence of confounding factors. It arises most noticeably in the literature review in studies of GP interventions because of the large number of potential factors apart from the one of interest within the studies which could plausibly have an effect on smoking behaviour. GP interventions can be thought of as having a 'package' of characteristics each of which may affect the outcome. These characteristics include: definition of the intervention; intensity of the intervention; single or multiple interventions; and existence and length of follow-up, each of which will affect the outcome.

For example Cockburn *et al.* (1992) set out to assess the cost-effectiveness of three different approaches to marketing a smoking cessation kit to Australian physicians. The kit was marketed by: personal delivery and explanation to GP by educational facilitator; delivery to receptionist by volunteer courier; and delivery to practice by mail. The kit is somewhat unusual in that it contains a two-tier strategy. Smokers are assessed and those most motivated to quit are assigned to an intensive intervention group which is more involved and personalised than the intervention received by the remainder. In addition each group were followed-up at six weeks to reinforce use of the kit. Evaluation took place at four months. However, the method of follow-up differed across the groups being by: personal visit; phone call; and letter respectively. There are thus three different marketing approaches, three different follow-up methods and two separate smoking interventions in this study, all of which can theoretically affect outcomes. It is therefore difficult to ascribe differences in outcome to the marketing approaches alone.

Another common issue that arises particularly in population-based studies is that of respondent bias:

- Respondent bias can arise where mass-media interventions advertise for 'registrants' to their campaigns and may result in biased results which are not generalisable to the target population.

- Awareness of possible respondent bias is important when generalising results.

Registrants are smokers who actively reply to some newspaper or other media invitation to register with a cessation campaign – this usually involves the mailing of self-help materials including manuals, smoking diaries and the like in return. Where surveys have been undertaken quit rates of registrants have been significantly higher (usually twice as great) as those in the general target population. Such registration may be inducing respondent bias, that is encouraging the smokers in the population who are more motivated, and therefore more likely to quit, to register and actively seek help with cessation.

The danger arises where studies which use surveys of registrants only (probably due to resource constraints) are generalised to the target population see, for example, Danaher *et al.* (1984). A series of short cessation programmes were televised on a local American network. Registrants were encouraged and received an advice brochure. At 12 months, 6.2 per cent of registrants and 2.4 per cent of the more general smoking population in the area remained abstinent. The registrants were likely to benefit from the brochure independently of the television campaign and be more motivated to quit than non-registrants. There may be, however, some additional benefits to such activity but these require careful evaluation.

Costs

This section is obviously relevant to cost-effectiveness studies only. A critical aspect in all such studies is the definition and measurement of costs:

- It is crucial to know what has been included and omitted from the cost figures reported in any cost-effectiveness study.

A good study will present a list of costs considered and usually provide a rationale for their inclusion or exclusion. An example is the study of Altman *et al.* (1987). This study analyses the cost-effectiveness of three cessation programmes from the Stanford Five Cities community heart disease programme. The following range of costs associated with the programmes are included: staff and staff benefits; overheads; rent; supplies and materials; travel; data analysis; and the participation time of smokers.

A knowledge of the costs omitted from a study is also important especially when comparing different levels of interventions. For example, if personnel costs are the only costs included, as in Green and Johnson's (1983) review of cost-effectiveness, large-scale and community programmes with substantial overheads may appear more cost-effective than small-scale single agency studies.

There are several categories of cost which are controversial in economic evaluation. The most significant in this context are the treatment of donated volunteer effort in face-to-face interventions such as the delivery of leaflets, of donated air-time in televised mass-media campaigns and the treatment of continuing programme development and evaluation costs.

Most studies reviewed below tend to disregard the costs associated with volunteers and donations. This is because the perspective taken is that of the sponsoring body. If society's perspective were taken such costs would probably be included, again see the example of McParlane *et al.* (1987) above. However, in certain circumstances there are arguments for including volunteer costs in a sponsoring agency's viewpoint. In order to implement a successful study in practice it may be infeasible to use volunteers, in which case the costs of volunteer time from the original study should be costed in some way. Similarly donated air time may have to be paid for if a campaign were aired nationally rather than locally or became a regular occurrence rather than a discrete event. On the other hand, Drummond (1980) has implicitly argued that because some voluntary labour is only offered for specific tasks, it cannot be used for another purpose and therefore has no opportunity cost. These arguments should be noted when assessing studies involving donated air time or volunteer labour. However, there are no strict rules for dealing with this issue and a subjective decision about how to deal with volunteer effort must be taken.

A similar conclusion holds for the treatment of development and evaluation costs associated with an intervention. The study of Altman *et al.* (1987) is a good example. The interventions were part of a long-term community heart disease prevention study. The interventions were also expected to be repeated in following years with some modification after evaluation. In this case the development and evaluation costs were included in the cost-effectiveness indicators. In general if the intervention is expected to be implemented and evaluated on a routine basis development and evaluation costs should be included since they are an integral part of the intervention. In other cases they should be disregarded.

(f) Outcomes

The main outcome measure used in smoking studies is quit rates. There are advantages which stem from this concentration on quit rates. Quit rates are a well-defined and easily measured concept although deception is a problem in studies which rely on self-reported smoking behaviour. Quitting is the ultimate target for smokers who no longer wish to smoke and is also the most desired medical outcome. A basic characteristic of health promotion is that any gains in lives saved or reductions in major smoking related-diseases from an intervention now will only become apparent in the distant future. This means that it is often impractical and prohibitively expensive to follow a cohort of smokers who receive an intervention and a control, to ensure low drop-out rates at follow-up and record the differences, if any, in final health outcomes. This means that most studies have used quit rates, and sometimes mean falls in daily cigarette consumption as the main outcome measure.

Fortunately, reasonably reliable epidemiological evidence does exist from large-scale studies which can be used to estimate likely final health outcomes, mainly in terms of mortality rates, for smokers, ex-smokers and never-smokers. A benefit of using the quit rate as an intermediate outcome measure is that it can be converted to final health outcomes, if desired, by making use of this stock of knowledge (see Townsend, 1993 for an example).

However, concentration on quit rates can lead to neglect of other relevant outcomes. For example, much of the publicity surrounding the smoking health scares in the 1950s and 1960s led not only to reductions in the prevalence of smoking but also a switch from high tar to low tar and filtered brands. Some health gains will result if smoking cessation interventions lead to reductions in daily cigarette consumption amongst smokers who, although subjected to the intervention, either relapse or do not quit in the first place. Several studies in this review have reported significant reductions in consumption associated with interventions (see Danaher *et al.* 1984; Wheeler, 1988; Abelin *et al.* 1989).

Another problem is the behaviour of those lost to the study. For example, over 8 per cent of the initial sample taken by Nørregaard *et al.* (1992) were lost to follow-up and as much as 20 per cent or more in other studies have been similarly lost. If the characteristics of those lost are different from those who remain, outcomes may also be different and external validity may be compromised. These issues are considered further in relation to cohort studies in Chapter 4, section 3.

There are several further issues associated with relapse. First, we do not fully understand the process of relapse itself. Although even temporary cessation is beneficial to health more research is needed to determine the key factors in relapse in order to design more effective and cost-effective interventions. Relapse also raises an important methodological point, the distinction between sustained abstinence quit rates and point prevalence quit rates:

- Sustained abstinence quit rates and point prevalence quit rates are the two major ways of assessing outcomes in face-to-face and population-based studies of smoking cessation. It is important to recognise when they are used and their key differences. Point prevalence quit rates are always higher for the same intervention and can suggest misleadingly good results.

The sustained abstinence quit-rate is stricter and measures what percentage of the study sample quit initially and stay quit till the end of the study period. Any relapse amongst subjects, despite any subsequent quitting, classifies them as smokers. High initial quit rates are whittled down due to attrition. At 12 months sustained quit rates are often as low as 2–10 per cent. This method has advantages in that those remaining quit to 12 months are less likely to relapse subsequently – it therefore provides good information about the cohort of core smokers that quit permanently due to an intervention. Point prevalence on the other hand is a cross-sectional measure, it does not follow a cohort of abstainers through time. Instead prevalence in the total sample is assessed at several discrete points in time. It therefore includes the present smoking status of both sustained abstainers and past or subsequent relapsers who at present are not smoking. As a consequence point prevalence rates are always higher than sustained quit rates. The advantage of this method is that it takes account of the majority of smokers who pass through a cycle of quitting and relapse, which sustained abstinence rates ignore. The disadvantage is that it is difficult adequately to assess the net effect of the intervention because of the combination of permanent and temporary quitters. A common solution is to include both as outcome measures where this is feasible.

Relapse also raises an important policy question: which is preferable on health and cost-effectiveness grounds, high short-term quit rates followed by significant relapse and low long-term permanent quitting or low but sustained initial quit rates? These alternatives imply different approaches to cessation. Until more studies link intermediate outcomes such as quit rates to final health outcomes such as life years gained or quality adjusted life years (QALYs) this important question is likely to remain unanswered.

Cost–effectiveness ratios

Cost-effectiveness ratios are generated by combining outcome data with the cost data which produced that outcome (see Tolley, 1993 for a detailed exposition). For example the outcome from a smoking campaign that cost the HEA £100 000 could be 2000 permanent ex-smokers after 12 months. Cost-effectiveness is therefore £50 per quitter. A less successful campaign could have rendered 1000 quitters at the same cost – cost-effectiveness is therefore £100 per quitter. Therefore,

- the higher the cost-effectiveness figure the lower the cost-effectiveness of the intervention.

Cost-effectiveness figures can be generated for process, intermediate and final health outcomes. For example, cost per anti-smoking leaflet delivered, cost per 12-month abstainer from an intervention and cost per life year gained from an intervention. In general final outcomes are extrapolated from intermediate outcomes and epidemiological evidence.

As Tolley (1993) outlines, there are three basic approaches to the presentation of cost-effectiveness results: the production of a 'baseline' estimate of the average costs per unit of outcome; assessment of the additional costs per extra unit of outcome for an expansion or contraction of an intervention; and modification of the 'baseline' to allow for differences in assumptions and in the timing of costs and benefits. This latter stage is also known as sensitivity analysis.

All the cost-effectiveness studies reviewed here produce some sort of 'baseline' estimates although some do not adequately explain the derivation or assumptions that lie behind their cost figures. Existing cost-effectiveness studies of smoking cessation and prevention concentrate on comparisons between two or more alternatives rather than assessing the incremental cost-effectiveness of expanding or contracting an existing one. This is mainly because smoking cessation programmes are discrete, they are rarely continuous and thus expansion or contraction is irrelevant. Exceptions are the study of Oster *et al.* (1986) who examine the incremental cost-effectiveness of prescribing nicotine gum as an adjunct to physicians' advice and Cummings *et al.* (1989) which measured the additional costs and effects on smoking prevalence of a follow-up visit for further advice. However, within a national smoking cessation programme incremental cost-effectiveness would be useful to guide the allocation of funds between existing campaigns and interventions. At present such a formal framework does not exist in the UK, although the HEA funds and carries out several campaigns annually and supports initiatives at local level.

Although 'baseline' cost-effectiveness figures represent the 'best' estimate of the cost-effectiveness of an intervention they are often fragile. Sensitivity analysis aims to discover how fragile and how generalisable study results are to other situations. This is done by varying the major assumptions implicit or explicit in a study, such as the effectiveness of the intervention and the cost of personnel or materials, and computing new cost-effectiveness figures for these different situations. A method often used is to combine several pessimistic or optimistic assumptions to produce worst case or best case scenarios respectively. These act as lower and upper bounds for the possible range of cost-effectiveness figures. A sensitivity analysis will identify the assumptions that have the greatest and least impact on cost-effectiveness. Good studies are defined as those where sensitivity analysis reveals that varying the basic assumptions has little impact on the results. These studies are therefore easily generalisable to other situations. Studies where varying the assumptions produces large and dramatic changes in results are less generalisable. Most analyses fall in the middle ground where some assumptions are fragile to change and others are not.

Obvious problems may arise in cost-effectiveness studies which use sensitivity analysis. First, not all relevant assumptions may be subjected to change. Second, sensitivity analyses are confusing and can be difficult to interpret correctly. This interpretation problem ironically increases with the number of assumptions questioned and thus the comprehensiveness of the study. Whilst 'baseline' results unambiguously indicate the most cost-effective option sensitivity analysis muddies the waters. This is because each alternative intervention will be associated with a range of cost-effectiveness figures depending on the changes in assumptions made. It is rare for these bands not to overlap in a comprehensive analysis. It is therefore conceivable that under different scenarios all of the alternatives will be cost-effective relative to the others. A judgement must be made as to the feasibility of the assumptions which result in different cost-effective rankings from that at 'baseline'. In most cases the 'baseline' result will remain the most likely cost-effective option since by definition the assumptions and results used in its calculation are the most realistic. However, in some instances where the results are close or where the result is very sensitive to small changes in particular assumptions a sensitivity analysis may overturn the cost-effectiveness rankings derived at 'baseline'. Although a sensitivity analysis adds some ambiguity to an economic evaluation this should be welcomed since in practice many factors decide the relative cost-effectiveness of different interventions and these are likely to change over time. Sensitivity analysis extends the relevance of a study to situations when these factors do change. It also provides information about the points where one intervention switches from being less cost-effective to more cost-effective than an alternative.

3. External validity

Most if not all of the caveats discussed in section 2 will affect external validity since a study which has poor internal validity is not representative of the true relationships between behavioural or health outcomes and the intervention. However, there are cases where an internally valid study may still have low external validity. This section is reserved for a discussion of instances when this could arise.

Generalisability

We have briefly discussed the three main types of study design in section 2(d). The main point is that as one moves from RCTs to non-experimental designs internal validity falls but external validity and generalisability in particular rises. RCTs are the most desired study design from an internal validity perspective but, ironically, the least desired from an external validity viewpoint because they are undertaken in unrealistic controlled settings:

- Generalising the results of trials to practice is problematical. RCT results are likely to overestimate the effectiveness and possible cost-effectiveness of an intervention.
- Account must be taken of the settings and circumstances where interventions will be used in practice as these will undoubtedly modify the effectiveness of interventions.

A good example is the generalisability of trials of nicotine chewing gum and transdermal nicotine patches (TNPs). Sanders (1992) summarises the results of twelve recent trials of nicotine replacement therapy. In clinic settings 12-month cessation rates of 31–63% were achieved for gum relative to 14–45% for placebo. However, in practice nicotine gum is likely to be used much more widely in GP settings or sold over the counter from pharmacies. The relevance of RCT results from clinic settings to actual practice is questionable. Hughes *et al.* (1989) undertook a study of gum versus placebo in a family practice setting, concluding that '... when used in a non-selected group of smokers with a brief intervention in a general medical practice, the pharmacological effects of nicotine gum to increase cessation are either small or non-existent.' TNPs are being widely marketed as over-the-counter aids to smoking cessation in the UK. However, the results of successful trials in the US indicates that adjuvant therapy as delivered by a physician is critical to their success. If the settings are different the results will be different. Walsh and Redman (1993) also discuss generalisability with respect to studies of smoking cessation during pregnancy.

This can also have knock-on effects for non-experimental studies. Non-experimental studies by definition do not generate effectiveness data. Effectiveness has to be estimated, by formal or informal means, from previous studies. However, non-experimental studies aim to assess effectiveness in real situations and this can cause problems if there is little information available except those from RCTs and/or in different settings. A good example is the aforementioned study of Oster *et al.* (1986). Their effectiveness data was largely based on trial results from clinic settings whereas their aim was the economic evaluation of nicotine gum in family practice settings. The fact that the cost-effectiveness results were most sensitive to the assumptions about effectiveness reinforces the uncertainty surrounding their results.

Another issue which arises from Chapter 5 is the discrepancy between cohort and cross-section results. Farquhar *et al.* (1990) report results from the Stanford Five Cities project, an extensive community-wide coronary heart disease risk reduction programme. Extensive evaluation was carried out by means of cross-sectional and cohort surveys in two intervention and two control cities. The cohort survey indicated a significant reduction in cigarette prevalence in the intervention cities relative to the controls. The cross-sectional results indicated no significant difference at each follow-up to five years post-intervention. Dwyer *et al.* (1986) report similar results in their analysis of the Sydney and Melbourne Quit for Life campaigns.

This discrepancy is important because it casts uncertainty on the results of at least two resource-intensive research studies. There are several possible explanations: each cross-sectional survey will include immigrants to the area who have not been subjected to all interventions; on the other hand cohort subjects will be subject to the full-scale campaign; behaviour change in the cohort may also be intensified by repeated follow-ups; finally those lost to follow-up from the survey tended to be current smokers, non-white and less-educated than average. It seems likely that cohort populations naturally mutate into older, non-smoking and more immobile populations over time. In contrast cross-section surveys pick-up dynamic changes in the population due to immigration and emigration.

The question of which survey results are more valid inevitably arises.

Cohort surveys are indispensable for tracking the final health outcomes associated with an intervention. However, whilst they also map out the full behaviour change, potential cross-sectional studies may be more valid in the generalisation of results to other populations. More research is needed to test the legitimacy of these propositions.

Comparability

The smoking cessation literature is varied and there are few accepted standard methods or procedures to be followed when conducting a study.

- Non-standardisation of methodology and outcome measures across studies is a considerable obstacle to comparability. It makes it difficult to draw unequivocal conclusions about the effectiveness of broadly similar interventions and restricts the usefulness of a wide body of knowledge.

This applies equally to face-to-face and population-based analyses. For example in a review of recent GP-based smoking cessation studies Sanders (1992) found that a 'brief intervention' in practice meant one or more of the following: brief advice; self-help booklets; nicotine and/or placebo gum; support from a smokers' clinic; follow-up letters; educational lectures; health visitor and nurse appointments; questionnaires; contracting quit dates with patients and counselling. Mass-media approaches also differ in the size and type of population targeted and in content, timing, duration and frequency of airing. All these factors reduce comparability.

Comparisons across countries are also difficult because of differences in culture and population characteristics; costing structures; health care arrangements; and media structures. Many US studies (McParlane *et al.*, 1987, for example) take the perspective of a voluntary health organisation (VHO) or health maintenance organisation (HMO). Comparable bodies do not exist in the UK and it is uncertain whether these perspectives are identical to that of provider units in the National Health Service. Similarly many mass-media interventions are broadcast, at zero or subsidised cost to the sponsor, over small localised television networks in the US (see Danaher *et al.*, 1984 and LeRoux and Miller, 1983 amongst others). It is doubtful whether such coverage could be as easily or cheaply generated in the UK, given the large size of even regional television stations in this country.

A problem common to face-to-face and population studies is the different follow-up periods used in otherwise similar studies. Twelve month sustained quit rates are most common for two reasons. First, an easily recognisable period such as a year may be thought of as a suitable target for abstention. Second, relapse is less frequent and subjects still quit after this period are more likely to be permanently ex-smokers. However, there are many studies which report only shorter-term results from as little as 6 weeks post-intervention. Whilst this information is valid in itself longer-term rates, to at least 12 months, should also be reported to aid comparability. There is the danger that high short-term headline rates may be incorrectly compared to lower but longer-term rates from similar or competing studies. This should be avoided.

A related issue is the comparability of some recent TNP studies. Both the studies of Tønnesen *et al.* (1991) and Abelin *et al.* (1989) reviewed in Chapter 2 define abstention in a much looser way than is standard in the rest of the smoking cessation literature. Abelin *et al.* allowed 1-3 cigarettes per week and Tønnesen *et al.* unlimited smoking for up to 24 hours followed by less than 15 per cent of previous daily intake between visits.

Several authors of cost-effectiveness studies reviewed in Chapter 2 argue that from their results smoking cessation compares well with other long-accepted medical practices. Whilst this may be true the authors do not present enough detail fully to support their claims. For example Oster *et al.* (1986) argue that nicotine gum as an adjuvant to physician advice costs up to $4500 per life year saved for middle-aged men whilst the pharmacological treatment of mild hypertension costs $11 300 and the treatment of elevated cholesterol levels $126 000 in the same age group. Care is needed in interpreting these figures. No information is given regarding sensitivity analysis, different discounting procedures, relevant costs included or the perspective taken in these studies.

- If authors are to argue that smoking interventions are cost-effective relative to other treatment options they must provide enough information to enable a valid comparison.

It is also arguable whether such highly aggregated and cursory comparisons are always that instructive. Such comparisons do not address the most practical alternatives to nicotine gum based cigarette cessation programmes, that is other cessation or treatment options. It is unlikely that many actual decision-makers would be in a position to act upon such information. What is more relevant is a comparison of the cost-effectiveness of different methods for reducing the number of smokers, information on which decision-makers can act at local level. They still need more data on the effectiveness and cost-effectiveness of alternative smoking cessation and prevention options. Wider considerations may be more helpful for political purposes in helping to shift priorities and resources into smoking health promotion (level 3 or 4) but do not tell us anything about which is the most cost-effective smoking intervention.

Meta-analysis

Several studies in our review use meta-analysis rather than traditional literature review techniques to pool and synthesise results from many studies (Lam *et al.*, 1981 and Viswesvaran and Schmidt, 1992, for example). Meta-analyses use formal statistical techniques to combine results from similar trials and studies in order to reach general conclusions. The objectivity of meta-analysis is seen as a great advantage over more subjective approaches such as literature reviews by its proponents but is criticised for making unjustified statistical assumptions and producing oversimplified results by its detractors (Thompson and Pocock, 1991).

Both views can be correct. Meta-analysis is a valuable tool providing an insight into the confusing and varied world of smoking cessation studies. However, it can produce misleading results if not applied cautiously and correctly. For more details see L'abbe *et al.* (1987), Sacks *et al.* (1987), Thompson and Pocock (1991), Delahaye *et al.* (1991), Spitzer (1991) and Kassirer (1992). There are several conditions which should be met if results from meta-analysis can be used with confidence:

- The validity of a meta-analysis is dependent on a lack of bias in its component studies. All the factors discussed under section 2 'Internal validity' will impart some bias.
- Meta-analysis assumes that the true effects of an intervention are identical for all studies, or fluctuate around a mean value. However, as we have seen smoking cessation studies are often heterogeneous by design.

Assigning lower weights in the statistical analysis to less internally valid studies will reduce their impact but such procedures are at present arbitrary and subjective. The homogeneity assumption implies that all study results reflect the same true effect and that observed differences across studies are due to chance alone. This is a strong assumption. There are formal tests which alert us to the existence of heterogeneity, although deciding what to do about it is more difficult. L'abbe *et al.* (1987) suggest that meta-analysis may be ill-advised in such circumstances.

- Meta-analyses will often indicate a significant net effect due to an intervention despite the fact that some component studies find no significant effect. Results from meta-analyses only give the average effects over all studies. Generalising to real settings rests on the assumption that the studies included are representative of all studies.

In conclusion, a valid meta-analysis can give clear guidelines about the likely effectiveness of different interventions. However, the conditions under which meta-analyses is valid are fairly restrictive. Since smoking cessation and prevention studies are by their nature heterogenous great care must be taken in carrying out and interpreting the results from studies which include meta-analytic techniques.

Conclusions

Results from studies of smoking cessation have an important role in guiding decisions of both purchasers and providers of health education interventions. Criteria are, however, required in order to assess critically the policy conclusions that can be drawn from a variety of studies undertaken with different interventions, in different time periods and in different countries. In this appendix aspects of both internal and external validity of studies of smoking cessation were explored within an economic framework.

It can be seen that smoking cessation is a particularly troublesome area because of its imprecise and psychological nature. It is consequently difficult to ensure either internal or external validity in practice. This implies that the results of smoking cessation studies should be treated with great care. Whilst a large stock of valuable knowledge exists it is still difficult to be precise about the effectiveness of competing interventions. This should be borne in mind when reading the text of this report.

Appendix B *Key effectiveness studies*

Chapter 2

Abelin, T., Buehler, A., Müller, P., Vesanen, K. and Imhof, P. (1989) 'Controlled trial of transdermal nicotine patch in tobacco withdrawal', *Lancet* no. 8628, pp.7–10.

Buchkremer, G., Minneker, E. and Block, M. (1991) 'Smoking cessation treatment combining transdermal nicotine substitution behavioral therapy', *Clinical Pharmacology and Therapeutics* **24**, 96–102.

Canadian Task Force on the Periodic Health Examination (1986) 'The periodic health examination: II. 1985 update', *Canadian Medical Association Journal* **134**, 724–7.

Chapman, S. (1990) 'General practitioner anti-smoking programmes: which one?' *Medical Journal of Australia* **15**, 508–9.

Covey, L. S. and Glassman, A. H. (1991) 'A meta-analysis of double-blind placebo-controlled trials of clonidine for smoking cessation', *British Journal of Addiction* **86**, 991–8.

Cummings, S. R., Hanson, B., Richard, R. J., Stein, M. J. and Coates, T. J. (1988) 'Internists and nicotine gum', *Journal of the American Medical Association* **260**, 1565–9.

Daughton, D. M., Heatley, S. A., Prendergast, J. J., Causey, D., Knowles, M., Rolf, C. N., Cheny, R. A., Hatelid, K., Thomson, A. B. and Rennard, S. I. (1991) 'Effect of transdermal nicotine delivery as an adjunct to low-intervention smoking cessation therapy: a randomized, placebo-controlled, double-blind study', *Archives of Internal Medicine* **151** (4), 749–52.

Elixhauser, A. (1990) 'The costs of smoking and cost effectiveness of smoking-cessation programs', *Journal of Public Health Policy*, Summer, pp. 218–37.

Evans, D. and Lane, D. S. (1980) 'Long-term outcome of smoking cessation workshops', *American Journal of Public Health* **70** 725–7.

Fiore, M. C., Jorenby, D. E., Baker, T. B. and Kenford, S. L. (1992) 'Tobacco dependence and the nicotine patch: clinical guidelines for effective use', *Journal of the American Medical Association* 268 (19), 2687–94.

Fiore, M. C., Novotny, T. E., Pierce, J. P., Giovino, G. A., Hatziandreu, E. J., Newcomb, P. A., Surawicz, T. S. and Davis, R. M. (1990)

'Methods used to quit smoking in the United States', *Journal of the American Medical Association* **263** (20), 2760–5.

Fiore, M. C., Pierce, J. P., Remington, P. C. and Fiore, B. J. (1990) 'Cigarette smoking: the clinician's role in cessation, prevention, and public health', *Disease-a-Month* **36** (4), 181–242.

Frankel, S. (1993) 'If you can stick it, you can kick it', *The Independent*, 18 January.

Gourlay, S. G. (1991) 'Tobacco smoking control,' *Lancet*, no. 8755, p. 1484.

Harris, M. E. (1983) 'Cigarette smoking among successive birth cohorts of men and women in the United States during 1900–1980', *Journal of the National Cancer Institute* **71** (3), 473–9.

Herbert, J. R., Kristeller, J., Ockene, J. K., Landon, J., Luippold, R., Goldberg, R. J. and Kalan, K. (1992) 'Patient characteristics and the effect of three physician-delivered smoking interventions', *Preventive Medicine* **21** (5), 557–73.

Hughes, J. R. (1986) 'Problems of nicotine gum', in Ockene, J. K. (ed.) *The Pharmacological Treatment of Tobacco Dependence: Proceedings of the World Conference*. Institute for the Study of Smoking Behavior and Policy, Cambridge, Mass., pp. 141–7.

Hughes, J. R., Gust, S. W., Keenan, R. M., Fenwick, J. W. and Healey, M. L. (1989) 'Nicotine vs placebo gum in general medical practice', *Journal of the American Medical Association* **261**, 1300–5.

Hughes, J. R., Wadland, W. C., Fenwick, J. W., Lewis, J. and Bickel, W. K. (1991) 'Effect of cost on the self-administration and efficacy of nicotine gum: a preliminary study', *Preventive Medicine* **20**, 486-96.

Hurt, R. D., Lauger, G. G., Offord, K. P., Kottke, T. E. and Dale, L. C. (1990) 'Nicotine-replacement therapy with use of a transdermal nicotine patch: a randomized double-blind placebo-controlled trial', *Mayo Clinical Proceedings* **65**, 1529–37.

Hwang, S. and Lee, L. (1992) 'Health: marketers and consumers get the jitters over severe shortage of nicotine patches', *Wall Street Journal*, 22 May.

Kottke, T. E., Battista, R. N., DeFriese, G. H. and Brekke, M. L. (1988) 'Attributes of successful smoking cessation interventions in medical practice', *Journal of the American Medical Association* **259**, 2883-9.

Lam, W., Sze, P. C., Sacks, H. S. and Chalmers, T. C. (1987) 'Meta-analysis of randomised controlled trials of nicotine chewing-gum', *Lancet* no. 8549, pp. 27–30.

Lancet (1991) 'Nicotine use after the year 2000', *Lancet* **337**, 1191–2. (Editorial.)

Mulligan, S. C., Masterson, J. G., Devane, J. G. and Kelly, J. G. (1990) 'Clinical and pharmacokinetic properties of a transdermal nicotine patch', *Clinical Pharmacology and Therapeutics* **47**, 331-7.

Owen, O. G. (1992) 'How well do nicotine patches work?' *General Practitioner*, 23 October, p. 38.

Pederson, L. L. (1982) 'Compliance with physician advice to quit smoking: a review of the literature', *Preventive Medicine* **11**, 71–84.

Prochazka, A. V., Petty, T. L., Nett, L., Silvers, G. W., Sachs, D. P., Rennard, S. I., Daughton, D. M., Grimm, R. H. and Heim, C. (1992) 'Transdermal clonidine reduced some withdrawal symptoms but did not increase smoking cessation', *Archives of Internal Medicine* **152** (10), 2056–69.

Rich, J. D. (1992) Letter to the editor, *New England Journal of Medicine* **326** (5), 344–5.

Richmond, R. L., Austin, A. and Webster, I. W. (1986) 'Three year evaluation of a programme by general practitioners to help patients to stop smoking', *British Medical Journal* **292**, 803–6.

Rose, J. E., Levin, E. D., Behm, F. M., Adivi, C. and Schur, C. (1990) 'Transdermal nicotine facilitates smoking cessation', *Clinical Pharmacology and Therapeutics* **47**, 323–30.

Russell, M. A. H., Merriman, R., Stapleton, J. and Taylor, W. (1983) 'Effect of nicotine chewing gum as an adjunct to general practitioner's advice against smoking', *British Medical Journal*, **287**, 1782–5.

Russell, M. A. H., Stapleton, J. A., Jackson, P. H., Hayek, P. and Belcher, M. (1987) 'District programme to reduce smoking: effect of clinic supported brief intervention by general practitioners', *British Medical Journal* **295**, 1240–44.

Russell, M. A. H., Wilson, C., Taylor, C. and Baker, C. D. (1979) 'Effect of general practitioners advice against smoking', *British Medical Journal* ii, 231–5.

Sanders, D. (1992) *Smoking Cessation Interventions: Is Patient Education Effective? A Review of the Literature*. Health Promotion Sciences Unit, Department of Public Health and Policy, Publication No. 6. London School of Hygiene and Tropical Medicine.

Schwartz, J. L. (1987) *Review and Evaluation of Smoking Cessation Methods: the United States and Canada, 1978–1985*. US Department of Health and Human Services, Public Health Service, National Institutes of Health, National Cancer Institute, Division of Cancer Prevention and Control. NIH Publication No. 87–2940.

Stoto, M. A. (1986) *Changes in Adult Smoking Behaviour in the United States 1955 to 1983*. Smoking Behavior and Policy Discussion Paper. Harvard University.

Sutherland, G., Stapleton, J. A., Russell, M. A. H., Jarvis, M. J., Hayek, M.J., Belcher, M. and Feyerabend, C. (1992) 'Randomised control trial of nasal nicotine spray in smoking cessation', *Lancet* **340**, 324–9.

Thompson, R. S., Michinich, M. E., Friedlander, L., Gilson, B., Grothaus, L. C. and Storer, B. (1988) 'Effectiveness of smoking cessation interventions integrated into primary care practice', *Medical Care* **26** (1), 62–76.

Tønneson, P., Nørregaard, J., Mikkelsen, K., Jorgensen, S. and Nilsson, F. (1993) 'A double-blind trial of a nicotine inhaler for smoking cessation', *Journal of the American Medical Association* **269** (10), 1268–71.

Tønnesen, P., Nørregaard, J., Simonsen, K. and Säwe, U. (1991) 'A double-blind trial of a 16-hour transdermal nicotine patch in smoking cessation', *New England Journal of Medicine* **325** (6), 311–15.

Transdermal Nicotine Study Group (1991) 'Transdermal nicotine for smoking cessation: six-month results from two multicenter controlled clinical trials', *Journal of the American Medical Association* **266** (22), 3133–8.

US Department of Health and Human Services (1988) *The Health Consequences of Smoking: Nicotine Addiction: a Report of the Surgeon General.* DHHS Publication No. (CDC) 88-8406. US Government Printing Office, Washington DC.

US Department of Health and Human Services (1989) *Reducing the Health Consequences of Smoking 25 Years of Progress: a Report of the Surgeon General.* DHHS Publication No. (CDC) 89-8411. US Government Printing Office, Washington DC.

Viswesvaran, C. and Schmidt, F. L. (1992) 'A meta-analytic comparison of the effectiveness of smoking cessation methods', *Journal of Applied Psychology* **77** (4), 554–61.

West, R. (1992) 'The "nicotine replacement paradox" in smoking cessation: how does nicotine gum really work?' *British Journal of Addiction* **87**, 165–7.

Wilson, D. M., Taylor, W., Gilbert, R., Best, J. A., Lindsay, E. A., Williams, D. G. and Singer, J. (1988) 'A randomized trial of a family physician intervention for smoking cessation', *Journal of the American Medical Association* **260**, 1570-4.

Chapter 3

Baric, L., Macarthur, C. and Sherwood, M. (1976) 'A study of health education aspects of smoking in pregnancy', *International Journal of Health Education* **19** (Sup), 1–17.

Bauman, K. E., Bryan, E. S., Dent, C. W. and Koch, C. G. (1983) 'The influence of observing carbon monoxide levels on cigarette smoking by public prenatal patients', *American Journal of Public Health* **73**, 1089–91.

Brenner, H. and Lielck, A. (1993) 'The role of childbirth in smoking cessation', *Preventive Medicine* **22**, 225–36.

Burling, T., Bieglow, G. E., Robinson, J. C. and Mead, A. M. (1991) 'Smoking during pregnancy: Reduction via objective assessment and directive advice', *Behaviour Therapy* **22**, 31–40.

Ershoff, D. H., Mullen, P. D. and Quinn, V. P. (1989) 'A randomized trial of a serialized self-help smoking cessation program for pregnant women in an HMO', *American Journal of Public Health* **79**, 182–7.

Hjalmarson, A. I., Hahn, L. and Svanberg, B. (1991) 'Stopping smoking during pregnancy: effect of a self-help manual in a controlled trial', *British Journal of Obstetrics and Gynaecology* **98**, 260–4.

Langford, E. R., Thompson, E. G. and Tripp, S. C. (1983) 'Smoking and health education: evaluation of a program for women in prenatal classes', *Canadian Journal of Public Health* **74**, 285–9.

Lilley, J. and Forster, D. P. (1986) 'A randomized controlled trial of individual counselling of smokers in pregnancy', *Public Health* **100**, 309–15.

Macarthur, C., Newton, M. R. and Knox, E. G. (1987) 'Effect of anti-smoking health education on infant size at birth: a randomised control trial', *British Journal of Obstetrics and Gynaecology* **94**, 295–300.

Mayer, J. P., Hawkins, B. and Todd, R. (1990) 'A randomized evaluation of smoking cessation interventions for pregnant women at a WIC clinic', *American Journal of Public Health* **80**, 76–9.

Messimer, S. R., Hickner, J. M. and Henry, R. C. (1989) 'A comparison of two antismoking interventions among pregnant women in eleven primary private care practices', *Journal of Family Practice*, **28**, 283–8.

Mullen, P. D., Quinn, V. P. and Ershoff, D. P. (1990) 'Maintenance of non-smoking postpartum by women who stopped smoking during pregnancy', *American Journal of Public Health* **80**, 992–4.

Olds, D. L., Henderson, C. R., Tatelbaum, R. and Chamberlain, R. (1986) 'Improving the delivery of prenatal care and outcomes of pregnancy: a randomised trial of nurse home visitation', *Paediatrics* **77**, 16–28.

Sexton, M. and Habel, J. R. (1984) 'A clinical trial of change in maternal smoking and its effect on birth weight', *Journal of the American Medical Association* **251**, 911–15.

Valbø, A. and Schioldborg, P. (1991) 'Smoking cessation in pregnancy: mode of intervention and effect', *Acta Obstetrica et Gynecologica Scandinavica* **70**, 309–13.

Walsh, R. and Redman, S. (1993) 'Smoking cessation in pregnancy: do effective programmes exist?' *Health Promotion International* **8** (2), 111–27.

Windsor, R. A., Cutter, G., Morris, J., Reese, J., Manzella, B., Bartlett, E. E., Samuelson, C. E. and Spanos, D. (1985) 'The effectiveness of smoking cessation methods for smokers in public health maternity clinics: a randomised trial', *American Journal of Public Health* **75**, 1389–92.

Windsor, R. A. and Orleans, C. T. (1986) 'Guidelines and methodological standards for smoking cessation research among pregnant women: improving the science and art', *Health Education Quarterly* **13**, 131–61.

Chapter 4

Altman, D. G., Flora, J. A., Fortmann, S. P. and Farquhar, J. W. (1987) 'The cost-effectiveness of three smoking cessation programs', *American Journal of Public Health* **77** (2), 162–5.

Atkinson, A. B. and Skegg, J. L. (1973) 'Anti-smoking publicity and the demand for tobacco in the UK', *The Manchester School* **41**, 265–82.

Ben-Sira, Z. (1981) 'Latent fear-arousing potential of fear-moderating and fear-neutral health promoting information', *Social Science and Medicine* **15**, 105–12.

Borren, P. and Sutton, M. (1992) 'Are increases in cigarette taxation regressive?' *Health Economics* **1**, 245–53.

Bosanquet, N. and Trigg, A. (1991) 'Smoking and economic incentives in Europe', *British Journal of Addiction* **86** (5), 627–30.

Clement, B. and Hall, C. (1993) 'Passive smoking victory may lead to cigarette ban', *The Independent*, 28 January.

Cockburn, J., Ruth, D., Silagy, C., Dobbin, M., Reid, Y., Scollo, M. and Naccarella, L. (1992) 'Randomised trial of three approaches for marketing smoking cessation programmes to Australian general practitioners', *British Medical Journal* **304**, 691–4.

Cornwell, R. (1993) 'Smoking report in US heralds new curbs', *The Independent*, January.

D'Ardis, M. (1986) *Report on International No Smoking Day: 12th March 1986*. Health Education Bureau, Dublin.

Department of Health (1992) *Effect of Tobacco Advertising on Tobacco Consumption: a Discussion Document Reviewing the Evidence*. Economics and Operational Research Division, Department of Health.

Donovan, R. J., Fisher, D. A. and Armstrong, B. K. (1984) 'Give it away for a day: an evaluation of Western Australia's first smoke free day', *Community Health Studies* **8** (3), 301–6.

Doxiadas, S. A., Trihopsulos, D. V. and Phylactou, H. D. (1985) 'Impact of a nationwide anti-smoking campaign'. *Lancet* no. 8457, pp. 712–13.

Dwyer, T., Pierce, J. P., Hannam, C. D. and Burker, N. (1986) 'Evaluation of the Sydney "Quit for Life" anti-smoking campaign, Part 2: Changes in smoking prevalence', *Medical Journal of Australia* **144**, 344–7.

Dyer, N. (1982) *Evaluating So You Want to Stop Smoking: Interim report*. British Broadcasting Corporation.

Dyer, N. (1983) Evaluating So You Want to Stop Smoking – Results of a Follow-up One Year Later. British Broadcasting Corporation.

Egger, G., Fitzgerald, W., Frape, G., Monaem, A., Rubinstein, P., Tyler, C. and Mckay, B. (1983) 'Results of large scale media antismoking campaign in Australia: North Coast Quit for Life programme', *British Medical Journal* **287**, 1125–8.

Eiser, J. R., Sutton, S. R. and Wober, M. (1978) 'Can television influence smoking?' *British Journal of Addiction* **73**, 215–19.

Engleman, S. (1987) 'The impact of mass media anti-smoking publicity', *Health Promotion* **2** (1), 63–74.

Farquhar, J. W., Fortmann, S. P., Flora, J. P., Barr Taylor, C., Haskell, W. L., Williams, P. T., Maccoby, N. and Wood, P. D. (1990) 'Effects of communitywide education on cardiovascular disease risk factors', *Journal of the American Medical Association* **264** (3), 359–65.

Flay, B. R. (1987a) *Selling the Smokeless Society*. American Public Health Association, Washington DC.

Flay, B. R. (1987b) 'Mass media and smoking cessation: a critical review', *American Journal of Public Health* **77**, 153–60.

Flay, B. R., Gruder, C. L., Warnecke, R. B. and Jason, L. A. (1987) *One Year Follow-up of the Chicago Televised Smoking Cessation Programme*.

Manuscript, University of Southern California.

Flynn, B. S., Worden, J. K., Secker-Walker, R. H., Badger, G. J., Geller, B. M. and Costanza, M. C. (1992) 'Prevention of cigarette smoking through mass media intervention and school programs', *American Journal of Public Health* **82** (6), 827–34.

Fry, V. and Pashardes, P. (1988) *Changing Patterns of Smoking: Are There Economic Causes?* Institute for Fiscal Studies Report Series No. 30. Institute for Fiscal Studies.

Fujii, E. T. (1980) 'The demand for cigarettes: further empirical evidence and its implications for public policy', *Applied Economics* **12**, 479–89.

Garrison, R. J., Gold, R. S., Wilson, P. W. F. and Kannel, W. B. (1993) 'Educational attainment and coronary heart disease risk: the Framingham Offspring Study', *Preventive Medicine* **22** (1), 54–64.

Gredler, B. and Kunze, M. (1981) 'Impact of a national campaign on smoking attitudes and patterns in Austria', *International Journal of Health Education* **24** (4), 271–9.

Hamilton, J. L. (1972) 'The demand for cigarettes: advertising, the health scare and the cigarette advertising ban', *Review of Economics and Statistics* **54**, 401–10.

Hauknes, A. (1981) Results from an evaluation of a special smoking and health information campaign in Norwegian newspapers and on television in 1977', in Leathar, D. S., Hastings, G. B. and Davies, J. K. (eds) *Health Education and Media*. Pergamon Press, Oxford.

Jason, L. A., Tait, E., Goodman, D. and Gruder, C. L. (1987) *Effects of a Television Cessation Intervention among Low Income and Minority Smokers*. Manuscript, De Paul University, Chicago.

Korhonen, H. J., Niemensivu, H., Piha, T., Koskela, K., Wiio, J., Anderson Johnson, C. and Puska, P. (1992) 'National TV smoking cessation program and contest in Finland', *Preventive Medicine* **21**, 74–87.

LeRoux, R. S. and Miller, M. E. (1983) 'Electronic media-based smoking cessation clinic in the USA', *International Journal of Health Education* **2** (1), 23–37.

Leu, R. E. (1984) 'Anti-smoking publicity, taxation, and the demand for cigarettes', *Journal of Health Economics* **3**, 101–16.

Lieberman Research Incorporated (1979–85) *A Study of the Impact of the Great American Smokeout: Report to the ACS*. American Cancer Society, New York.

McAlister, A. and Sunderland, B. (1986) *Ways to Really Stop Smoking: Final Report, Pilot Program*. Sunderland and Associates, Houston, Texas.

Macaskill, P., Pierce, J. P., Simpson, J. M. and Lyle, D. M. (1992) 'Mass media-led antismoking campaign can remove the education gap in quitting behavior, *American Journal of Public Health* **82** (1), 96–8.

Maccoby, N. (1980) 'Promoting positive health-related behavior in adults', in *Proceedings of the Fourth Vermont Conference on Primary Prevention of Psychopathology: Promoting Competence and Coping during Adulthood*. University Press of New England, Hanover, New England.

Mogielnicki, R. P., Neslin, S., Dulac, J., Balestra, D., Gillie, E. and Corson, J. (1986) Tailored media can enhance the success of smoking cessation clinics', *Journal of Behavioral Medicine* **9** (2), 141–61.

O'Byrne, D. J. and Crawley, H. D. (undated) *Conquest Smoking Cessation Campaign*. Health Education Bureau, Dublin.

Pekurinen, M. (1989) 'The demand for tobacco products in Finland', *British Journal of Addiction* **84** (10), 1183–92.

Peto, J. (1974) 'Price and consumption of cigarettes: a case for intervention?' *British Journal of Preventive and Social Medicine* **28**, 241–5.

Pierce, J. P., Macaskill, P. and Hill, D. (1990) 'Long-term effectiveness of mass media led antismoking campaigns in Australia', *American Journal of Public Health* **80** (5), 565–9.

Porter, F. (1969) 'Assessing public reactions to an anti-smoking campaign', *Ontario Medical Review*, pp. 217–21.

Puska, P., Koskela, K., McAlister, A., Pallonen, U., Vartiainen, E. and Homan, K. (1979) 'A comprehensive television smoking cessation programme in Finland', *International Journal of Health Education* **22** (4 supp), 1–29.

Puska, P., Salonen, J., Nissinen, A. Tuomilehto, J., Vartiainen, E., Korhonen, H., Tanskanen, A., Ronqvist, P., Koskela, K. and Huttunen, J. (1983) 'Change in risk factors for coronary heart disease during 10 years of a community programme (North Karelia Project)', *British Medical Journal* **287**, 1840–4.

Puska, P., McAlister, A., Pekkola, J. and Koskela, K. (1981) 'Television in health promotion: evaluation of a national programme in Finland', *International Journal of Health Education* **24** (4), 2–14.

Puska, P., Tuomilehto, J., Salonen, J. and Nissinen, A. (1981) *Community Control of Cardiovascular Diseases: The North Karelia Project*. World Health Organization, Copenhagen.

Puska, P., Wiio, J., McAlister, A., Koskela, K., Smolander, A., Pekkola, J. and Maccoby, N. (1985) 'Planned use of mass media in national health promotion: The 'Keys to Health' TV program in 1982 in Finland', *Canadian Journal of Public Health* **76**, 336–42.

Raw, M. and Van der Plight, J. (1981) 'Can television help people stop smoking?' in Leathar, D.S., Hastings, G. B. and Davis, J. K. (eds) *Health Education and the Media*. Pergamon Press, Oxford.

Reid, R. and Smith N. (1991) *What is the Single Most Important Intervention for the Prevention of Smoking-related Disease?* Based on paper presented at Seventh World Conference on Tobacco and Health, Perth, Western Australia: 1–5 April 1990.

Research Bureau Limited (1972) *Anti-smoking Advertising: Report on the Evaluation Research*. Health Education Council.

Research Services Limited (1973) *Report on Cinema Campaign*. Health Education Council.

Roberts, D. F. and Maccoby, N. (1984) 'Effects of mass communication', in Lindzey, G. and Aronson, E. (eds) *Handbook of Social Psychology*

Addison-Wesley, Reading, Mass.

Sallis, J. F., Hill, R. D., Killen, J. D., Telch, M. J., Flora, J. A., Girard, J. and Taylor, C. B. (1986) 'Efficacy of self-help behavior modification materials in smoking cessation', *American Journal of Preventive Medicine* **2** (6), 342–4.

Saunders, G. (1978) 'Smokers Quitline', in Schwartz, J. L. (ed) *Progress in Smoking Cessation*. Proceedings of the International Conference on Smoking Cessation, June 1978. American Cancer Society, New York.

Schneider, L., Klein, B. and Murphy, K. (1981) 'Government regulation of cigarette health information', *Journal of Law and Economics* **24**, 575–612.

Sumner, H. T. (1971) 'The demand for tobacco in the UK', *The Manchester School* **39**, 23–7.

Townsend, J. (1984) 'Cost-effectiveness', in Crofton, J. and Wood, M. (eds) *Smoking Control: Strategies and Evaluation in Community and Mass Media Programmes*. Ulster Cancer Foundation/Health Education Council.

Warnecke, R. B., Langenberg, P., Wong, S. C., Flay, B. R. and Cook, T. D. (1992) 'The Second Chicago Televised Smoking Cessation Program: a 24 month follow-up', *American Journal of Public Health* **82** (6), 835–40.

Warner, K. E. (1977) 'The effects of the Anti-smoking Campaign on cigarette consumption', *American Journal of Public Health* **67** (7), 645–50.

Warner, K. E. (1981) 'Cigarette smoking in the 1970s: the impact of the Anti-smoking Campaign on cigarette consumption. *Science* **211**, 729–31.

Wheeler, R. J. (1988) 'Effects of a community-wide smoking cessation programme', *Social Science and Medicine* **27** (12), 1387–92.

Witt, S. F. and Pass, C. L. (1981) 'The effects of health warnings on the demand for cigarettes', *Scottish Journal of Political Economy* **28**, 86–91.

Appendix C *Estimation and source of cost data*

1. Cost estimates

Table C.1 shows derived estimates of costs for each intervention from four different perspectives, those of the GP, the wider sponsor, the smoker and society. The table clearly shows precisely which inputs have been costed. The range of costs given indicates the best and worst case scenarios regarding costs. These are dependent on different assumptions regarding: average or timed consultations, the inclusion/exclusion of overheads and quit rates and therefore dosage and cost of TNPs and nicotine gum. This is not traditional sensitivity analysis as such but an allowance for the considerable uncertainty about how to cost GP services in particular. These figures are reproduced in Table 5.4 in the main text and derived in section 2 below. Section 3 lists relevant source material.

2. Deriving the cost estimates

The cost estimates are derived according to the perspectives of the GP, the smoker, the intervention sponsor and society. The cost of scenarios 1 to 4 has been calculated on a per-smoker basis. These costs have been multiplied by 11 914 400, the estimated number of total smokers in England and Wales in 1993.* In contrast the cost of scenarios 6 and 7 has been estimated directly from details on total expenditure for various campaigns in the literature and from the Health Education Authority.

The GP perspective

Costs associated with GPs are one of the key costs to be measured given their inclusion in interventions 1 to 4, where the GP is the main conduit for advice and counselling and the source of most additional material. It is therefore important that the opportunity cost of a GP's time is measured accurately. In theory the correct value attached to GP time should vary across the different options outlined above since opportunity cost refers to the value of the best alternative use of the GP's time. In practice however wages and salaries are often used as a proxy. The justification for this is that at the margin the cost of an additional GP employed by a health authority

---

*The number of smokers was estimated from data on prevalence from the *General Household Survey 1992* (OPCS, 1994) and from data on the size of the adult population from *Population Trends*. Interpolation was used to derive the 1993 estimate.

should equal the marginal benefits which flow to society as a consequence of that employment (Hughes, 1991).

There is no generally accepted method for costing GP consultations. Previous attempts have been made although these tend to concentrate on the costs of an *average* consultation. Hughes (1991) develops more general guidelines for costing consultations. Recent Government Expenditure Plans have also included some information on the costs of an average GP consultation. Cost estimates vary quite significantly depending on the price year and source. This is because the definition of an 'average consultation' and the costs that it incurs differ widely across studies. Hughes (1991) rightly argues that where GP's time is likely to be a major part of the cost of the consultation an accurate estimate of the length of consultation is important. In most circumstances the cost associated with a smoking intervention will not resemble an average consultation because the time to deliver the intervention will be different.

Intervention 1: Opportunity cost of GP's time

Below we take two approaches to derive upper and lower bound estimates of the costs associated with GP time and possible practice overheads. This involves two different estimating procedures. The first to derive an upper bound of the costs incurred is to divide total gross general medical service costs by total number of consultations. We take the Treasury's (1992) estimate of £10.87 per consultation in 1991–2 at 1992–3 prices. However, we adjust it to take account of the large difference in time and thus costs between a surgery and home consultations. From the *General Household Survey 1992* (OPCS, 1994) we know the ratio of home to surgery consultations and from DHSS/General Medical Survey (1987) the average consultation time at home and in the surgery. Based on Coyle (1993):

Defining:

$$ATC = (ASCC \times \%S) + (AHCC \star \%H) \tag{1}$$

and assuming:

$$AHCC = ASCC \times THC\ /\ TSC \tag{2}$$

we can rearrange for ASCC:

$$ASCC = ATC\ /\ ((\%H \times (THC\ /\ TSC)) + \%S) = \underline{£8.98} \tag{3}$$

Key

ATC   =   average total consultation cost (£10.87)
ASCC   =   average surgery consultation cost
AHCC   =   average home consultation cost
S   =   proportion of consultations which take place at the surgery (0.89)
H   =   proportion of consultations which take place at the home (0.11)
THC   =   average time of a home consultation
TSC = average time of a surgery consultation

Table C.1: Cost of smoking cessation interventions

Intervention	Perspective	Costed inputs	Best and worst case cost estimates
1.	GP	1 minute opp. cost	£4 467 900 – £14 773 856
	Smoker	1 minute opp. cost	£1 036 553
	Sponsor	None	None
	Society	GP + smoker	£5 504 453 – £15 810 409
2.	GP	3 minutes opp. cost	£13 403 700 – £44 321 568
	Smoker	3 minutes opp. cost + 3 months gum if quit, 1 month if do not	None
	Sponsor	None	£326 943 051 – £434 887 515
	Society	GP + smoker	£371 264 619 – £448 291 215
3.	GP	1 minute opp. cost + 4 pre-arranged consultations costs	£162 961 132 – £442 739 104
	Smoker	(4 × travel costs) + (4 × 13 minutes + 1 minute opp. cost)	£48 855 712
	Sponsor	Printed cessation material	£23 828 800
	Society	GP + smoker + sponsor	£235 375 644 – £515 423 616
4.	GP	3 minutes opp. cost	£13 403 700 – £44 321 568
	Smoker	3 minutes opp. cost + 3 months TNPs if quit, 1 month if do not	£442 241 957 – £690 910 099
	Sponsor	None	None
	Society	GP + smoker	£486 563 525 – £704 313 799
5.	n.e.	n.e.	n.e.
6.	GP	n.a.	?
	Smoker	?	?
	Sponsor	Assumed to cost as much as the media component of full-weight national community campaign	£5 000 000
	Society	Sponsor + smoker	?

No.	Role	Description	Value
7.	GP		n.a.
	Smoker		?
	Sponsor	All costs involved in promotion, publicity and staging	£500 000
	Society	Sponsor + estimated costs to local health authorities costs to local health authorities	£1 000 000
8.	GP		n.a.
	Smoker		?
	Sponsor	Costs of production	£20 000
	Society		?
9.	GP		?
	Smoker		?
	Sponsor	All costs involved in promotion, publicity and staging	£10 000 000
	Society	Sponsor + supporting community events	£20 000 000
10.	GP		n.a.
	Smoker		?
	Sponsor	All costs for brief TV commercial and consequent distribution	£1 000 000
	Society		?

n.e: not estimated; n.a: not applicable; ?: costing relevant but conceptually and/or practically difficult; opp.: opportunity; TNP: transdermal nicotine patch.

Equation (1) defines average total consultation cost as the sum of home and surgery average costs weighted for their proportion of total visits. Equation (2) allows the elimination of average home consultation cost by assuming that the costs differ to surgery costs only by the amount of time involved. Finally equation (3) rearranges for average surgery consultation costs. We know that the average surgery consultation took 7.22 minutes in 1987. Assuming this figure is unchanged we can derive an average brief smoking consultation cost for 1992–3 from equation (3) (assuming such a consultation takes 1 minute). This figure includes *all* GP overheads and therefore acts as an upper bound for the costs associated with a GP smoking intervention consultation. *Upper bound (inc. overheads): £1.16 per minute.*

In the case of a brief intervention (such as advice) specific visits to the GP will not be made. Rather advice will be opportunistic and is dispensed within a pre-arranged consultation. Hughes (1991) argues that if a procedure requires an increase in the existing workload of ancillary staff these costs should be included. Similarly if it requires extra buildings or reallocation of space then overheads become a relevant cost. For brief advice dispensed incrementally during a pre-arranged consultation additional overheads will not be incurred. We thus assume that the only cost incurred is that of a GP's time. The average GP works a 38-hour week for 9 out of 10 weeks at an average salary of £40 010 (from 1 April 1992). This implies: *Lower bound (exc. overheads): £0.375 per minute.*

Intervention 2: Additional costs of follow-up appointments

For more intensive interventions or follow-ups separate appointments are deemed necessary. This implies both more GP time and additional administrative expenses. In addition if such appointments are structured through health promotion clinics additional costs will be involved associated with practice nurses and possible building alterations. Alternatively if an extra GP is required by the practice then his income (including allowance for overheads etc.) would be a reasonable proxy for the costs incurred to the practice. We concentrate on GP delivery of interventions, assume that no extra GPs are required and that additional overheads will not be incurred. Again two alternative approaches are considered. First, the upper bound estimate assumes that a follow-up/ intensive intervention will consist of an average GP consultation. We have estimated this to be £8.98 (equation (3) above). *Upper bound (inc. overheads): £8.98 per consultation, total of 4 consultations: £35.92.*

The lower bound estimate is again a more bottom–up approach. In this case we assume that the costs incurred include additional GP time and additional administrative expenses. Administrative expenses are assumed to be those mainly associated with secretarial duties. In 1990 there were 1.6 whole-time equivalent (wte) ancillary staff per GP in the UK (Department of Health, 1992c) of which two-thirds (1.07 wtes) were secretarial staff and/or receptionists. We assume that the same proportion of their time is taken up in administrative duties as is that of the GP in giving advice, etc. We further assume the average relevant employee is grade 3 in the middle band increment and again that the average consultation lasts 7.22 minutes. This implies £0.375 per GP per minute plus a further £0.085 per minute due to administration charges. Therefore average surgery consultation costs (inc. administration overheads) are £0.46 per minute. *Lower bound (inc. administration overheads): £3.32 per consultation, total of 4 consultations: £13.28.*

The smoker's perspective

The opportunity cost of patients' time is usually approximated by their salary or wages. This assumes that all patients are paid employees and that they are free to set their hours of work so that at the margin the value of the first unit of leisure is equal to the last unit of work. If patients see their GP during work hours the cost to them is their sacrificed wages, if they see the GP during their leisure time the cost is therefore equivalent. The same argument applies if the smoker is taking part in a community smoking cessation programme or watching media campaigns on the television. In practice however these assumptions do not hold. First, many patients are not in paid employment and secondly most of those who are are unable to pick and choose their hours of work and leisure.

Interventions 1 to 4: Opportunity cost of smoker's time

We approximate the opportunity cost of smoker's time in a different fashion because of the strictness of these two conditions and because of the practical difficulties involved in estimation on this basis. However, our alternative also entails making several restrictive assumptions. First it is assumed that smoking households have similar income characteristics to the average UK household. This is unlikely to be true since a higher than representative proportion of smokers come from lower socio-economic groups. However, ignoring this the Family Expenditure Survey gives details of average gross weekly household income and number of adults in the household. Dividing one by the other results in the average gross weekly income per adult from all sources. In practice some adults are part-time workers (particularly women), unpaid household workers (again particularly women), unemployed, retired or otherwise economically inactive. The next assumption is that despite this variance the 'average' adult derives this 'average' income from an average 38 hours of work or equivalent. This assumption could be reconciled if this 'equivalent' activity is valued in a similar fashion to the income from working. However, we admit it is a restrictive assumption. The opportunity cost associated with missing work or sacrificing leisure is therefore the value of this income per time period. The assumed total time period per week to which opportunity cost pertains is therefore 38 hours, in 1991 the mean gross income per adult per household per week was £197.85. This implies that the opportunity cost per smoker's minute was £0.087 in 1991. *Assumed/estimated opportunity cost of smoker: £0.087 per minute.*

Intervention 2: Travelling costs and further opportunity costs

For brief advice delivered by a GP additional travelling costs do not have to be calculated because the advice is assumed to take place during a pre-arranged consultation. However, for follow-up visits and more intensive interventions additional travel costs are likely to be incurred. A Royal Commission Report on the NHS (1979) revealed that over 80 per cent of patients live within 1 mile of their GP in urban areas and over 40 per cent lived within 1 mile in the most inaccessible area, West Cumbria. If we assume that all patients travel 1 mile by private transport travelling costs are estimated to be £0.37 (1992–3). In addition smokers travelling for a specific appointment will also incur additional opportunity costs during travel and during waiting for attention in the surgery. We assume an average speed of 20 mph during travel to the surgery which implies an additional 3 minutes opportunity cost plus an average waiting time of 10 minutes. *Assumed/estimated travel costs of smoker: £0.37. Assumed/estimated additional opportunity cost of smoker's time for more intensive interventions: £1.50 per consultation, total of 4 consultations £6.00.*

Interventions 3 and 4: The costs of nicotine gum and TNPs

Neither nicotine gum nor TNPs is available on NHS prescription in the UK. Therefore the costs associated with their use will fall mainly on the smokers themselves. We assume below that a prescription will be issued at the end of a pre-existing consultation. Nicotine gum is available on private prescription (no VAT payable on purchase) and over the counter at pharmacies. The most widely available brand is Nicorette (2 mg) in boxes of 30 and 105 pieces. The current retail price in the UK is £5.25 for the smaller size and £14.90 for the larger box. We assume that GPs will offer all their smoking patients a private prescription, which reduces the cost to £4.47 and £12.08 respectively. Oster *et al.* (1986), in their study of gum cost-effectiveness, reviewed the literature concerning average dosages of 2 mg Nicorette and found that 12-month quitters used an average 6 pieces per day for four months and assume that non-successful users consume only one month's worth at a similar rate. We make the same assumptions below in arriving at the cost to the smoker of a nicotine gum prescription. In addition all smokers will receive 3 minutes' consultation time (Oster *et al.* 1986). *Assumed/estimated gum cost for quitter: £84.56 (7 boxes of 105 pieces). Assumed/estimated gum cost for unsuccessful user: £24.16 (2 boxes of 105 pieces). Assumed/estimated opportunity cost per GP consultation for nicotine gum (3 min): £0.261*

Similar calculations apply to transdermal nicotine patches. Again we assume that it takes 3 minutes on average for a GP to deliver brief advice and a private prescription. Again TNPs are not available on NHS prescription but are available as a private subscription. The retail price of TNPs varies depending on brand but a recommended full-course lasting approximately three months costs £150–£185 including VAT (QUIT, 1993). On private prescription this cost falls to £127.66 – £157.45. As with nicotine gum we assume that unsuccessful users will use and purchase only one month's supply, therefore: *Assumed/estimated cost per successful quitter: £127.66–157.45. Assumed/estimated cost per unsuccessful user: £42.55–52.48. Assumed/estimated cost per GP consultation for TNPs (3 min): £0.261*

The NHS/sponsor's perspective

Intervention 1, 2, 4
These interventions are assumed to incur no costs from the NHS/ sponsor's perspective.

Intervention 3: The cost of cessation materials
Most studies of intensive interventions have used printed materials. In the United States much material is standardised and printed material provided by bodies such as the American Lung Association is used in many studies. In the UK the situation is different. Equivalent organisations such as the Imperial Cancer Research Fund concentrate on researching the disease implications of smoking and have less of an active preventive role. Bodies such as Action on Smoking and Health (ASH) and QUIT produce some material but the Health Education Authority is the main provider at a national level. Around 5000 free leaflets and guides are provided annually to local district health authorities which distribute them in hospitals and GP practices. The HEA sells printed cessation material to companies and distributes them to smokers on an individual basis. The HEA produces four main leaflets/booklets and also produces a resource list on smoking education (Health Education Authority, 1992), which provides details of self-help materials produced by other organisations. The most relevant publications are produced by organisations such as Exeter Health Promotion Department, Stop Smoking and QUIT. They tend to produce short, cheap guides costing from £0.15 to £1.35 per copy. More commercial material in the form of various books are also available but these are more expensive costing around £4.50 on average and up to £9.95 per copy. This material is unlikely to be issued by GPs. The cost estimates for printed cessation materials are therefore amongst the most difficult to quantify. We assume that smokers will receive each of the HEA guides plus the most expensive similar guide (£1.35), a total of £2.00 worth of printed materials. However, we realise that this is an extremely sensitive and unjustified assumption. *Cost of guides: £2.00.*

Intervention 6: Information campaigns
Information campaigns are likely to be aired as television commercials or possibly cinema commercials (Research Bureau, 1972; Research Services, 1973). As such costs to the sponsor will be considerably higher than for a cessation programme. However, very little information exists about the costs of a national information campaign. *We assume that a national information campaign will cost about half as much as the media component of a full-*

weight campaign, about £10 000 000. This reflects the fact that it is unlikely to be accompanied by much non–media supporting activity and be of lower intensity.

Intervention 7: Costs of National No Smoking Day

No Smoking Day (NSD) is the most widely known media–based smoking intervention which takes place in the UK. It is not at present possible to estimate with any degree of confidence the costs to society that NSD incurs. We assume that costs to GPs are negligible (although some increased activity may be expected if smokers are spurred into seeking advice about quitting). Reid *et al.* (1992) estimate that National NSD costs the national organising committee about £500 000 per annum. *Total estimated costs for NSD: £500 000.*

Intervention 8: TV cessation clinics

The major costs of a TV cessation programme fall into two categories: costs of production and costs of transmission. The recent Yorkshire TV cessation programme 'The Last Cigarette' cost approximately £20 000 to produce (personal communication, Yorkshire TV). In many cases programmes are either aired free of charge, or purchased by the BBC and ITV network. The HEA 'Health Show' broadcast in 1992 is one such example (personal communication, HEA Advertising Department). Transmission costs are borne by the television networks. The ITV network recoups the costs involved by selling commercial airtime around the programme. At present the ITV and BBC networks can provide no estimates relating to the costs of transmitting a smoking cessation programme nationwide. Therefore total cost estimates from society's point of view are omitted. *We assume that from the NHS/sponsor's perspective costs amount to £20 000.* Thus the costs of airing a dedicated programme are much lower than those of a series of commercials from a sponsor's perspective. However, the audience is likely to be lower.

Intervention 9: Costs of a media supported community-wide campaign

Again the wide variety of costs associated with a national TV campaign are likely to be underestimated. We again know very little about the opportunity costs to smokers or costs incurred by voluntary and local organisations. However, the recent advertising costs associated with the HEA's experimental 'Family Campaign' which features a number of cessation advertisements on prime-time TV has cost an estimated £1 600 000 in 1992–93. However, these are screened only in the northern TV regions. Reid *et al.* (1992) have estimated that a full-scale national campaign could cost in the region of £10 000 000. This does not seem unreasonable.

Intervention 10: Media promotion of cessation kits

This option is problematical to cost for two reasons: the variety of methods available to advertise and distribute kits, and the fact that few campaigns have been evaluated or costed. Altman *et al.* (1987) report the costs of a local newspaper campaign to advertise kits in the US but similar evaluations have not been carried out in the UK. NOP Market Research (1985a,b,c) have, however, evaluated a national exercise in 1985 carried out by the then Health Education Council. This consisted of a brief 30-second commercial and statement of details about how to register for a cessation kit. Total costs were reported as £750 000. We assume that costs have risen to approximately £1 000 000 for a similar exercise today.

It must be recognised that there are many possible options available to purchasers when advertising and distributing self-help kits. This is bound to lead to considerable doubt about the applicability of any estimated cost figure. Ideally specific and thorough economic evaluations would be carried out.

Society's perspective

If all relevant costs to the GP, the smoker and the intervention sponsor have been measured accurately and there are no further externalities to third parties then the cost to society for each intervention is merely the summation of GP, smoker and sponsor costs. In reality costs will not be measured accurately and there will be externalities. This is particularly true for media-based interventions because many costs are incurred by other agencies (such as voluntary organisations) which are usually never assessed or even acknowledged. The costs presented for society should therefore be treated as particularly tentative. For two of the interventions estimates of further societal costs are presented.

Intervention 7: National No Smoking Day
NSD also imposes costs on participating health authorities or voluntary organisations. Unpaid press coverage is also a cost to society and smokers' exposure to the advertisements should ideally be costed. These costs are difficult to measure. *However, Speller (1991)* estimates that at least an extra £500 000 is incurred by district health authorities.*

Intervention 9: Costs of a media-supported community-wide campaign
Further activities will also be involved in more extensive community-wide campaigns. Farquhar *et al.* (1990) found that media costs accounted for 50 per cent of total campaign costs. Assuming that this cost is incurred by other organisations implies an additional cost to society of £10 000 000. *Cost of community campaign: £10 000 000.*

---

*Personal communication from Donald Reid.

3. Data sources

GP salary
Intended average net remuneration.
Anonymous (1993) 'NHS fees and allowances', *Medeconomics* **14** (2), 117.

GP working time
Average total time spent on general medical services. Average of four surveys and *General Household Survey* (OPCS, 1992, 1994) data studying GP's workload in the UK.
Thomas, K., Birch, S., Milner, P., Nicholl, J., Westlake, L. and Williams, B. (1989) 'Estimates of general practitioner workload: a review', *Journal of the Royal College of General Practitioners* **39**, 509–13.

GP administration costs
Average hourly rate of grade 3 GP ancillary staff member in middle of increment scale, adjusted for average of 1.07 wte members per GP.
Anonymous (1992) 'Staff pay', *Medeconomics* **13** (7), 98.

Opportunity cost of smoker's time
Mean gross income per adult per household.
Calculated from Dennis, G. (1992) *Annual Abstract of Statistics 1993*. HMSO.
Original data derived from the Family Expenditure Survey.

Travel costs
Total standing and running costs, based on 10 000 miles average annual mileage for petrol car of 1001–1400 cc (April 1993).
AA Technical services (1993) *Motoring Costs*.

Distance from home to GP surgery
Based on survey results of patient's access to GP services as part of 1976 Royal Commission report on the National Health Service.
Royal Commission on the National Health Service (1979) *Access to Primary Care*. Research Paper No. 6. HMSO.

REFERENCES

Abelin, T., Buehler, A., Müller, P., Vesanen, K. and Imhof, P. (1989) 'Controlled trial of transdermal nicotine patch in tobacco withdrawal', *Lancet* no. 8628, pp.7–10.

Altman, D. G., Flora, J. A., Fortmann, S. P. and Farquhar, J. W. (1987) 'The cost-effectiveness of three smoking cessation programs', *American Journal of Public Health* **77** (2), 162–5.

Best, J. A. (1980) 'Mass media, self-management and smoking modification', in Davidson, P. O. and Davidson, S. M. (eds) *Behavioral Medicine: Changing Health Lifestyles*. Bruner/Mazel, New York.

Brenner, H. and Lielck, A. (1993) 'The role of childbirth in smoking cessation', *Preventive Medicine* **22**, 225–36.

Buck, D., Godfrey, C., Hardman, G. and Tolley, K. (1994) *Assessing the Cost-effectiveness of Health Promotion: Coronary Heart Disease*. Centre for Health Economics, University of York.

Callum, C., Johnson, K. and Killoran, A. (1992) *The Smoking Epidemic: A Manifesto for Action in England*. Health Education Authority.

Canadian Task Force on the Periodic Health Examination (1986) 'The periodic health examination: II. 1985 update', *Canadian Medical Association Journal* **134**, 724–7.

Cockburn, J., Ruth, D., Silagy, C., Dobbin, M., Reid, Y., Scollo, M. and Naccarella, L. (1992) 'Randomised trial of three approaches for marketing smoking cessation programmes to Australian general practitioners', *British Medical Journal* **304**, 691–4.

Cohen, S., Stookey, G., Katz, B., Drook, C. and Smith, D. (1989) 'Encouraging primary care physicians to help smokers quit: a randomised control trial', *Annals of Internal Medicine* **110** (8), 648–52.

Cox, J. L. and Mckenna, J. P. (1990) 'Nicotine gum: does providing it free in a smoking cessation program alter success rates? *Journal of Family Practice* **31** (3), 278–80.

Coyle, D. (1993) *Measuring Unit Costs*, mimeo. Centre for Health Economics, University of York.

Culyer, A. J. (1980) *The Political Economy of Social Policy*. Martin Robertson, Oxford.

Cummings, S. R., Hanson, B., Richard, R. J., Stein, M. J. and Coates, T. J. (1988) 'Internists and nicotine gum', *Journal of the American Medical Association* **260**, 1565–9.

Cummings, S. R., Rubin, S. M. and Oster, G. (1989) 'The cost-effectiveness of counseling smokers to quit', *Journal of the American Medical Association* **261** (1), 75–9.

Danaher, B. G., Berkanovic, E. and Gerber, B. (1984) 'Mass media based health behavior change: televised smoking cessation program', *Addictive Behaviors* **9**, 245–53.

Delahaye, F., Landrivon, G., Ecochard, R. and Colin, C. (1991) 'Meta-analysis', *Health Policy* **19**, 185–96.

Department of Health (1992a) *The Health of the Nation: a Strategy for Health in England*, Cm 1986. HMSO.

Department of Health (1992b) *Effect of Tobacco Advertising on Tobacco Consumption: a Discussion Document Reviewing the Evidence.* Economics and Operational Research Division, Department of Health.

Department of Health (1992c) *Statistics for General Medical Practitioners in England and Wales 1980–90. Statistical Bulletin* **4** (2) 92. Department of Health.

Department of Health and Social Security/General Medical Services Committee (1987) *General Medical Practitioners' Workload. A Report Prepared for the Doctors' and Dentists' Review Body 1985/6.* DHSS.

Dickinson, J. A., Wiggers, J., Leeder, S. R. and Sanson-Fisher, R. W. (1989) 'General practitioners' detection of patients' smoking status', *Medical Journal of Australia* **150**, 420–6.

Doxiadas, S. A., Trihopsulos, D. V. and Phylactou, H. D. (1985) 'Impact of a nationwide anti-smoking campaign', *Lancet* no. 8457, pp. 712–13.

Drummond, M. F. (1980) *Principles of Economic Appraisal in Health Care.* Oxford University Press.

Duncan, C., Stein, M. J. and Cummings, S. R. (1991) Staff involvement and special follow-up time increases physician's counseling about smoking cessation: a controlled trial', *American Journal of Public Health* **81** (7), 899–901.

Dwyer, T., Pierce, J. P., Hannam, C. D. and Burker, N. (1986) 'Evaluation of the Sydney "Quit for Life" anti-smoking campaign, Part 2: Changes in smoking prevalence', *Medical Journal of Australia* **144**, 344–7.

Dyer, N. (1982) *Evaluating So You Want to Stop Smoking: Interim Report.* British Broadcasting Corporation.

Dyer, N. (1983) *Evaluating So you want to stop smoking – Results of a Follow-up One Year Later.* British Broadcasting Corporation.

Engleman, S. (1987) 'The impact of mass media anti-smoking publicity', *Health Promotion* **2** (1), 63–74.

Ershoff, D. H., Quinn, V. P., Dolan Mullen, P. and Lairson, D. R. (1990) 'Pregnancy and medical cost outcomes of a self-help prenatal smoking cessation program in a HMO', *Public Health Reports* **105** (4), 340–7.

Evans, D. and Lane, D. S. (1980) 'Long-term outcome of smoking cessation workshops', *American Journal of Public Health* **70**, 725–7.

Farquhar, J. W., Fortmann, S. P., Flora, J. P., Barr Taylor, C., Haskell, W. L., Williams, P. T., Maccoby, N. and Wood, P.D. (1990) 'Effects of communitywide education on cardiovascular disease risk factors', *Journal of the American Medical Association* **264** (3), 359–65.

Fiore, M. C., Jorenby, D. E., Baker, T. B. and Kenford, S. L. (1992) 'Tobacco dependence and the nicotine patch: clinical guidelines for effective use', *Journal of the American Medical Association* **268** (19), 2687–94.

Fiore, M. C., Novotny, T. E., Pierce, J. P., Giovino, G. A., Hatziandreu, E. J., Newcomb, P. A., Surawicz, T. S. and Davis, R. M. (1990a) 'Methods used to quit smoking in the United States', *Journal of the American Medical Association* **263** (20), 2760–5.

Fiore, M. C., Pierce, J. P., Remington, P. C. and Fiore, B. J. (1990b) 'Cigarette smoking: the clinician's role in cessation, prevention, and public health', *Disease-a-Month* **36** (4), 181–242.

Flay, B. R. (1987a) *Selling the Smokeless Society*. American Public Health Association, Washington DC.

Flay, B. R. (1987b) 'Mass media and smoking cessation: a critical review', *American Journal of Public Health* **77**, 153–60.

Flynn, B. S., Worden, J. K., Secker-Walker, R. H., Badger, G. J., Geller, B. M. and Costanza, M. C. (1992) 'Prevention of cigarette smoking through mass media intervention and school programs', *American Journal of Public Health* **82** (6), 827–34.

Fry, J. (1993) *General Practice: The Facts*. Radcliffe Medical Press, Oxford.

Garrison, R. J., Gold, R. S., Wilson, P. W. F. and Kannel, W. B. (1993) 'Educational attainment and coronary heart disease risk: the Framingham Offspring Study', *Preventive Medicine* **22** (1), 54–64.

Godfrey, C. and Maynard, A. (1988) 'Economic aspects of tobacco use and taxation policy', *British Medical Journal* **297**, 339–43.

Godfrey, C. (1989) 'Factors influencing the consumption of alcohol and tobacco: the use and abuse of economic models', *British Medical Journal* **84** (10), 1123–38.

Godfrey, C. (1993) 'Banning tobacco advertising: can economists contribute to the debate?' *Health Economics* **2** (1), 1–5.

Godfrey, C., Edwards, H., Raw, M. and Sutton, M. (1993) *The Smoking Epidemic: A Prescription for Change*. Health Education Authority.

Gredler, B. and Kunze, M. (1981) 'Impact of a national campaign on smoking attitudes and patterns in Austria', *International Journal of Health Education* **24** (4), 271–9.

Green, L. W. (1977) 'Evaluation and measurement: some dilemmas for health education', *Journal of Public Health* **67**, 155–61.

Green, L. W. and Johnson, K. W. (1983) 'Health education and health promotion', in D. Mechanic (ed.) *Handbook of Health, Health Care, and the Health Professions*, pp. 744–65, Free Press, New York.

Gunning-Schepers, L. (1989) 'The health benefits of prevention: a simulation approach', Health Policy **12** (1-2), 1–255.

Harris, M. E. (1983) 'Cigarette smoking among successive birth cohorts of men and women in the United States during 1900–1980', *Journal of the National Cancer Institute* **71** (3), 473–9.

Hauknes, A. (1981) 'Results from an evaluation of a special smoking and health information campaign in Norwegian newspapers and on television in 1977', in Leathar, D. S., Hastings, G. B. and Davies, J. K. (eds) *Health Education and Media*. Pergamon Press, Oxford.

Health Education Authority (1992) *Smoking Education Resource List*. HEA.

Hughes, D. (1991) 'Costing consultations in general practice: towards a standardized approach', *Family Practice* **8** (4), 388–93.

Hughes, J. R. (1986) 'Problems of nicotine gum', in Ockene, J. K. (ed.) *The Pharmacological Treatment of Tobacco Dependence: Proceedings of the World Conference*. Institute for the Study of Smoking Behavior and Policy, Cambridge, Mass., pp.141–147.

Hughes, J. R., Gust, S. W., Keenan, R. M., Fenwick, J. W. and Healey, M. L. (1989) 'Nicotine vs placebo gum in general medical practice', *Journal of the American Medical Association* **261**, 1300–5.

Hughes, J. R., Wadland, W. C., Fenwick, J. W., Lewis, J. and Bickel, W. K. (1991) 'Effect of cost on the self-administration and efficacy of nicotine gum: a preliminary study', *Preventive Medicine* **20**, 486–96.

Hwang, S. and Lee, L. (1992) 'Health: marketers and consumers get the jitters over severe shortage of nicotine patches', *Wall Street Journal* 22 May.

Kassirer, J. P. (1992) 'Clinical trials and meta-analysis – what do they do for us? *New England Journal of Medicine* **327** (4), 273–4.

L'abbe, K. A., Detsky, A. S. and O'Rourke, K. (1987) 'Meta-analysis in clinical research', *Annals of Internal Medicine* **107**, 224–33.

Lam, W., Sze, P. C., Sacks, H. S. and Chalmers, T. C. (1987) Meta-analysis of randomised controlled trials of nicotine chewing-gum', *Lancet* no. 8549, pp. 27–30.

Lancet (1991) 'Nicotine use after the year 2000', *Lancet* **337**, 1191–2. (Editorial.)

Lando, H. (1975) 'Successful treatment of smokers with a broad-spectrum behavioral approach', *Journal of Consulting and Clinical Psychology* **43**, 350–5.

LeRoux, R. S. and Miller, M. E. (1983) 'Electronic media-based smoking cessation clinic in the USA', *International Journal of Health Education* **2** (1), 23–37.

Li, C. Q., Windsor, R. A., Lowe, J. B. and Goldenberg, R. L. (1992) 'Evaluation of the impact of dissemination of smoking cessation methods on the low birthweight rate and on health care costs: achieving year 2000 objectives for the nation', *American Journal of Preventive Medicine* **8** (3), 171–7.

Lilley, J. and Forster, D. P. (1986) 'A randomized controlled trial of individual counselling of smokers in pregnancy', *Public Health* **74**, 309–15.

Macarthur, C. Newton, M. R. and Knox, E. G. (1987) 'Effect of anti-smoking, health education on infant size at birth: a randomised control trial', *British Journal of Obstetrics and Gynaecology* **94**, 295–300.

Macaskill, P., Pierce, J. P., Simpson, J. M. and Lyle, D. M. (1992) 'Mass media-led antismoking campaign can remove the education gap in quitting behavior', *American Journal of Public Health* **82** (1), 96–8.

Madely, R. J., Gillies, P. A., Power, F. L. and Symonds, E. M. (1989) 'Nottingham Mothers Stop Smoking Project – baseline survey of smoking in pregnancy', *Community Medicine* **11** (2), 124–30.

Marks, J. S., Koplan, J. P., Hogue, C. J. R. and Dalmat, M. E. (1990) 'A cost-benefit/cost-effectiveness analysis of smoking cessation for pregnant women', *American Journal of Preventive Medicine* **6** (5), 282–9.

Mason, J., Drummond, M. and Torrance, G. (1993) 'Some guidelines on the use and abuse of cost-effectiveness league tables', *British Medical Journal* **306**, 570–2.

McGuire, A., Henderson, J. and Mooney, G. (1988) *The Economics of Health Care*. Routledge.

McGuire, C. (1992) *Pausing for Breath: a Review of No Smoking Day Research 1984–1991*. Health Education Authority.

McParlane, E. C., Dolan-Mullen, P. and DeNino, L. A. (1987) 'The cost effectiveness of an education outreach representative to OB practitioners to promote smoking cessation', *Patient Education and Smoking* 9, 263–4.

McPhee, S. J., Bird, J. A., Fordham, D., Rodnick, J. E. and Osborn, E. H. (1991) 'Promoting cancer prevention activities by primary care physicians', *Journal of the American Medical Association* **266** (4), 538–44.

NOP Market Research Limited (1985a) *Kathy: 1*. Health Education Council.

NOP Market Research Limited (1985b) *Kathy 2: Evaluation of the Campaign*. Health Education Council.

NOP Market Research Limited (1985c) *Overall Review of the Kathy Campaign*. Health Education Council.

Nørregaard, J., Tønnesen, P., Simonsen, K., Petersen, and Säwe, U. (1992) 'Smoking habits in relapsed subjects from a smoking cessation trial after one year', *British Journal of Addiction* **87**, 1189–94.

OPCS (1992) *General Household Survey 1988*. HMSO.

OPCS (1994) *General Household Survey 1992. HMSO*.

Oster, G., Delea, T. E. and Colditz, G. A. (1988). 'Maternal smoking during pregnancy and expenditures on neonatal health care', American Journal of Preventive Medicine **4** (4), 216–19.

Oster, G., Huse, D. M., Delea, T. E. and Colditz, G. A. (1986) 'Cost-effectiveness of nicotine gum as an adjunct to physician's advice against cigarette smoking', *Journal of the American Medical Association* **256** (10), 1315–18.

Owen, O. G. (1992) 'How well do nicotine patches work?' *General Practitioner*, 23 October, p. 38.

Parsonage, M. and Neuberger, H. (1991) *Discounting and QALYs*. Paper presented at the Health Economists' Study Group, Aberdeen.

Parsonage, M. and Neuberger, H. (1992) 'Discounting and health benefits', *Health Economics* **1** (1), 71–5.

Pederson, L. L. (1982) 'Compliance with physician advice to quit smoking: a review of the literature', *Preventive Medicine,* **11**, 71–84.

Phillips, C. J. and Prowle, M. J. (1993) 'Economics of a reduction in smoking: case study from Heartbeat Wales', *Journal of Epidemiology and Community Health* **47**, 215–23.

Pierce, J. P., Fiore, M. C., Novotny, T. E., Hatziandreu, E. J. and Davis, R. M. (1989) 'Trends in cigarette consumption in the United States: projections to the year 2000', *Journal of the American Medical Association* **261** (1), 61–5.

Prochaska, J. O. and DiClemente, C. C. (1983) 'Stages and processes of self-change in smoking: towards an integrative model of change', *Journal of Consulting and Clinical Psychology* **51**, 390–5.

QUIT (1993) *Which Way to Quit Smoking: a Consumer's Guide.* QUIT.

Reid, D. J., Killoran, A. J., McNeill, A. D. and Chambers, J. S. (1992) 'Choosing the most effective health promotion options for reducing a nation's smoking prevalence', *Tobacco Control* **1**, 185–97.

Reid, D. J., McNeill, A. D. and Glynn, T. J. (1994) 'Reducing the prevalence of smoking in youth: an international review'. (In press).

Reid, R. and Smith N. (1991) *What is the Single Most Important Intervention for the Prevention of Smoking-related Disease?* Based on paper presented at Seventh World Conference on Tobacco and Health, Perth, Western Australia: 1–5 April 1990. (Unpublished.)

Research Bureau Limited (1972) *Anti-smoking Advertising: Report on the Evaluation Research.* Health Education Council.

Research Services Limited (1973) *Report on Cinema Campaign.* Health Education Council.

Richmond, R. L., Austin, A. and Webster, I. W. (1986) 'Three year evaluation of a programme by general practitioners to help patients to stop smoking', *British Medical Journal* **292**, 803–6.

Roberts, D. F. and Maccoby, N. (1984) 'Effects of mass communication', in Lindzey, G. and Aronson, E. (eds) *Handbook of Social Psychology.* Addison-Wesley, Reading, Mass.

Rosén, M. and Lindholm, L. (1992) 'The neglected effects of lifestyle interventions in cost-effectiveness analysis', *Health Promotion International* **7** (3), 163–9.

Royal Commission on the National Health Service (1979) *Access to Primary Care.* Research Paper Number 6. HMSO.

Russell, M. A. H., Wilson, C., Taylor, C. and Baker, C. D. (1979) 'Effect of general practitioners advice against smoking', *British Medical Journal* ii, 231–5.

Sacks, H. S., Berrier, J., Reitman, D., Ancona-Berk, V. A. and Chalmers, T. (1987) 'Meta-analyses of randomized control trials', *New England Journal of Medicine* **316** (8), 450–5.

Sanders, D. (1992) *Smoking Cessation Interventions: Is Patient Education Effective? A Review of the Literature',* Health Promotion Sciences Unit, Department of Public Health and Policy, Publication No. 6. London School of Hygiene and Tropical Medicine.

Saul, H. (1993) 'Chancing your arm on nicotine patches', *New Scientist*, February 13.

Schwartz, J. L. (1987) *Review and Evaluation of Smoking Cessation Methods: the United States and Canada, 1978–1985*. US Department of Health and Human Services, Public Health Service, National Institutes of Health, National Cancer Institute, Division of Cancer Prevention and Control. NIH publication no. 87-2940.

Sexton, M. (1986) 'Smoking'. In Chamberlain, G. V. P. and Lumley, J. (eds) *Prepregnancy Care*. John Wiley, Chichester.

Shipp, M., Croughan-Minihane, M. S., Petitti, D. B. and Washington, A. E. (1992) 'Estimation of the break-even point for smoking cessation programs in pregnancy', *American Journal of Public Health* **82** (3), 383–90.

Spitzer, W. (1991) 'Meta meta-analysis: unanswered questions about aggregating data', *Journal of Clinical Epidemiology* **44** (2), 103–7.

Stoto, M. A. (1986) *Changes in Adult Smoking Behaviour in the United States 1955 to 1983*. Smoking Behavior and Policy Discussion Paper. Harvard University.

Thompson, S. G. and Pocock, S. J. (1991) 'Can meta-analyses be trusted?' *The Lancet* **338**, 1127–30.

Tolley, K. (1993) *Health Promotion: How to Measure Cost-effectiveness*. HEA.

Tønnesen, P., Nørregaard, J., Simonsen, K. and Säwe, U. (1991) 'A double-blind trial of a 16-hour transdermal nicotine patch in smoking cessation', *New England Journal of Medicine* **325** (5), 311–15.

Townsend, J. (1986) 'Cost-effectiveness and mass media programmes of smoking control', in Crofton, J. and Wood, M. (eds) *Smoking Control: Strategies and Evaluation in Community and Mass Media Programmes*. Ulster Cancer Foundation/Health Education Council.

Townsend, J. (1993) 'Policies to halve smoking deaths', *Addiction* **88**, 37–46.

Transdermal Nicotine Study Group (1991) 'Transdermal nicotine for smoking cessation: six-month results from two multicenter controlled clinical trials', *Journal of the American Medical Association* **266** (22), 3133–8.

Treasury (1992) *The Government's Expenditure Plans 1993–4 to 1995–6: Department of Health and Office of Population Censuses and Surveys*, Cm 2212. HMSO.

US Department of Health and Human Services (1991) *Strategies to Control Tobacco Use in the United States: a Blueprint for Public Health in the 1990s*. NIH Publication No. 92-3316. US Government Printing Office, Washington DC.

US Department of Health and Human Services (1994) *Preventing Tobacco Use among Young People: a Report of the Surgeon General*. Office on Smoking and Health, Centers for Disease Control and Prevention, Atlanta, Georgia.

Valbø, A. and Schioldborg, P. (1991) 'Smoking cessation in pregnancy: mode of intervention and effect', *Acta Obstetrica et Gynecologica Scandinavica* **70**, 309–13.

Velicer, W. F. and DiClemente, C. (1993) 'Understanding and intervenng, with the total population of smokers', *Tobacco Control* **2**, 95–6.

Viswesvaran, C. and Schmidt, F. L. (1992) 'A Meta-analytic comparison of the effectiveness of smoking cessation methods', *Journal of Applied Psychology* **77** (4), 554–61.

Walsh, R. and Redman, S. (1993) 'Smoking cessation in pregnancy: do effective programmes exist?' *Health Promotion International* **8** (2), 111–27.

Warner, K. E. (1977) 'The effects of the Anti-smoking Campaign on cigarette consumption'. *American Journal of Public Health* **67** (7), 645–50.

Warner, K.E. (1981) Cigarette Smoking in the 1970s: The impact of the Anti-smoking Campaign on cigarette consumption. *Science* **211,** 729–31.

Warner, K. E. and Cutter, G. R. (1988) 'A cost-effectiveness analysis of self-help methods for pregnant women', *Public Health Reports* **103** (1), 83–8.

Wells, K. B., Lewis, C. E., Leake, B., Schleiter, M. K. and Brook, R. H. (1986) 'The practices of general and subspeciality internists in counseling about smoking and exercise', *American Journal of Public Health* **6**, 1009–13.

Weshler, H., Levine, S., Idelson, R. K., Rohman, M. and Taylor, J. O. (1983) 'The physician's role in health promotion – a survey of primary-care practitioners', *New England Journal of Medicine* **308** (2), 97–100.

Wheeler, R. J. (1988) 'Effects of a community-wide smoking cessation programme', *Social Science and Medicine* **27** (12), 1387–92.

Williams, A. (1987) 'Screening for risk of CHD: Is it a wise use of resources?' in Oliver, M., Ashley-Miller, M. and Wood, D. *Screening for Risk of Coronary Heart Disease*. John Wiley.

Wilson, D.M., Taylor, W., Gilbert, R., Best, J. A., Lindsay, E. A., Williams, D. G. and Singer, J. (1988) 'A randomized trial of a family physician intervention for smoking cessation', *Journal of the American Medical Association* **260**, 1570–4.

Windsor, R. A., Cutter, G., Morris, J., Reese, J. Manzella, B., Bartlett, E. E., Samuelson, C. E. and Spanos, D. (1985) 'The effectiveness of smoking cessation methods for smokers in public health maternity clinics: a randomised trial', *American Journal of Public Health* **74**, 1389–92.

Windsor, R. A., Lowe, J. B., Perkins, L. L. Smith-Yoder, D., Artz, L., Crawford, M., Amburgy, J. and Boyd Jr, N. R. (1993a) 'Health education for pregnant smokers: its behavioral impact and cost benefit', *American Journal of Public Health* **83** (2), 201–6.

Windsor, R. A., Li, Q. L., Lowe, J. B., Perkins, L. L., Ershoff, O. and Glynn, T. (1993b) 'The dissemination of smoking cessation methods for pregnant women: achieving the year 2000 objectives', *American Journal of Public Health* **83** (2), 173–8.

Windsor, R. A. and Orleans, C. T. (1986). 'Guidelines and methodological standards for smoking cessation research among pregnant women: improving the science and art', *Health Education Quarterly* **13**, 131–61.